GOOD FRIDAY'S GOOD NEWS

BRIAN GRENIER CFC

GOOD FRIDAY'S GOOD NEWS

St Paul Publications

ACKNOWLEDGEMENTS

Texts taken from *New Revised Standard Version Bible*, copyright © 1989, by the Division of Christian Education of the National Council of the Churches of Christ in the USA. Used with permission.

GOOD FRIDAY'S GOOD NEWS

© Brian Grenier CFC, 1992

First published, October 1992

National Library of Australia
Cataloguing in Publication Data
Grenier, Brian
Good Friday's Good News
Bibliography
ISBN 1 875570 09 8
1. Jesus Christ — Passion — Biblical teaching. 2. Jesus Christ — Crucifixion — Biblical teaching. 3. Bible, N.T. John — Criticism, interpretation, etc. 4. Good Friday. I. Title. (Series: Faith and Prayer Education; 9).
232.96

Cover illustration: Crucifix in St Stephen's Cathedral, Brisbane, by John Elliot. Photograph reproduced by permission of *The Catholic Leader*.

Cover design: Bruno Colombari SSP

Published by
ST PAUL PUBLICATIONS — Society of St Paul,
60-70 Broughton Road — (PO Box 230) — Homebush, NSW 2140

Typeset and printed by Society of St Paul, Wantirna South, Victoria

St Paul Publications is an activity of the Priests and Brothers of the Society of St Paul who proclaim the Gospel through the media of social communication.

To Charles Hill

Contents

Introduction

Every year, during the Roman Catholic liturgical celebration of Good Friday, the passion narrative from St John's Gospel is proclaimed. Usually this reading is done in dramatic fashion with various roles being assigned to members of the congregation. On the preceding Sunday one of the Synoptic accounts of Jesus' passion will have been read in accordance with a three-year cycle which follows the sequence: Matthew (Year A), Mark (Year B) and Luke (Year C).

All of the above-mentioned Gospel readings are rather lengthy; and for this reason many celebrants, in my experience, preach very briefly (if at all) on Passion Sunday or on Good Friday. In any case, they argue, the texts themselves speak more eloquently and touch the human heart more surely than the words of the most able homilist.

While there is, I believe, some wisdom in this approach, it would be a pity if opportunities were not provided at other times for the members of the parish community to nurture their faith and inform their prayer by reflective study of the four passion narratives. To this end, one of these narratives might be chosen each year for special attention (perhaps during the Lenten season) in keeping with the triennial cycle of readings. As it is read every year, there is something to be said for beginning this series with the Johannine account of Jesus' passion.

With these observations in mind, I have set out in this small book to make available to the non-specialist reader some of the insights of contemporary biblical scholarship with respect to chapters 18 and 19 of St John's Gospel. My hope is that it will facilitate understanding of the sacred text, stimulate prayerful reflection on it and assist all who participate in the dramatic reading of the Gospel on Good Friday.

Reading the sacred scriptures

From experience we know that we do not bring the same level of attentiveness to the various materials we read from day to day. We do not read a legal contract, a novel, a letter from a loved one, a menu, a newspaper, or a magazine in a dentist's waiting-room in the same way. One item calls for close scrutiny; another invites us to browse.

Even when we take up our Bible, it makes quite a difference whether we intend to read it academically (as an object of study), contemplatively (as a resource for prayer) or contextually (as a source of moral guidance and prophetic judgment). Ideally these three approaches to Sacred Scripture should be mutually supportive rather than mutually exclusive, as indeed they will be if we are in the habit of reading the Bible not only with our physical eyes but also with the eyes of faith.

However we plan to read it, we should open our Bible with great reverence, conscious of the real presence of God in the inspired words of Scripture just as we are conscious of the real presence of Jesus, our risen Saviour, in the Holy Eucharist. Both are food for the journey we are making as God's pilgrim people. As the Second Vatican Council reminds us in the Dogmatic Constitution on Divine Revelation (Flannery 1975:762):

> *The Church has always venerated the divine Scriptures as she venerated the Body of the Lord, in so far as she never ceases, particularly in the sacred liturgy, to partake of the bread of life and to offer it to the faithful from the one table of the Word of God and the Body of Christ* (Dei Verbum 21).

Reading the passion narratives

Let us picture some of the more influential disciples of Jesus in their chosen place of refuge on the evening of his crucifixion. Though we call that day 'Good Friday', they would have been hard pressed to find anything positive in it. Sad, fearful and disillusioned, they piece together the information they have managed to collect about the arrest, trials, torture and public execution of the one in whom they had invested their hopes. What a different narrative of Jesus' passion and death we would have today if our only written record of those events had been composed that evening.

Fortunately, this is not the case. We are blessed in the joyful possession of no fewer than four accounts of the climactic moments of our Lord's earthly life. Written decades after the events they record and in the light of Jesus' resurrection from the dead on Easter Sunday, they provide us with far more than a mere chronicle of what took place. They are documents of faith, human in expression but divine in inspiration, in which historical detail is subservient to theological truth. In reading them we should not lose sight of these facts as fundamentalist Christians are wont to do.

The Johannine story of the passion

At first glance (and with good reason), it would appear that the gloom of Good Friday has given way to the joyful reassurance of Easter rather more completely in the Gospel according to St John than in the Synoptic Gospels. However, a closer reading of the Johannine text should bring home to us how frequently the evangelist alludes to the events of Jesus' passion and death.

Even in the prologue of his Gospel, John, by speaking of a light shining confrontationally in the darkness (1:5), prepares his readers for the eventual rejection of Jesus by his own people (1:11).[1] When Jesus first appears on the scene, the Baptist identifies him as 'the Lamb of God' (1:29,36; cf. 19:36) — an image which has sacrificial overtones (cf. Is 53:7; 1 Cor 5:7; 1 Pet 1:18-19). Jesus speaks of himself several times as 'the Son of Man [who must be] lifted up' (3:14; 8:28; 12:32). 'He said this', the evangelist adds by way of commentary, 'to indicate the kind

---

1 When we read the Fourth Gospel, we need to remember that it was written at a time of vigorous polemic between Jews and Christians. This coloured John's treatment of the passion and death of Jesus and, over the centuries, provided specious grounds for some Christians to indulge in anti-Semitic behaviour. Let us, therefore, take note of Vatican II's Declaration on the Relation of the Church to Non-Christian Religions (Flannery 1975:741): 'Neither all Jews indiscriminately at that time, nor Jews today, can be charged with the crimes committed during his passion' (*Nostra Aetate* 4). In Brown's (1986:12) opinion: 'Not Jewish background but religious mentality is the basic component in the reaction to Jesus.' For further pertinent comment, see Kaufman (1991).

of death he was to die' (12:33). From repeated references we know that this death by crucifixion will take place only when Jesus' 'hour' has come (2:4; 7:6-8,30; 8:20; 12:23,27; 13:1; 17:1).

We could also point to Jesus' prediction concerning the destruction and raising up in three days of 'the temple of his body' (2:19-22); to the statement of his willingness, as the good and loving shepherd, to lay down his life for his sheep (10:11,15,17-18; cf. 15:13); to the determined efforts of the authorities to arrest him (7:32,45; 10:39; 11:57) and to the corresponding vigilance of Jesus to avoid capture (7:1,10-11; 8:59; 10:39; 12:36; 11:54; cf. 7:30; 8:20); to his confrontations with those who would stone him to death for 'blasphemy' (8:59; 10:31-33; cf. 5:18; 7:1,19,25; 8:37; 11:8); to Caiaphas's plan, in response to the popular support for Jesus occasioned by the raising to life of Lazarus, 'to have one man die for the people' (11:50); and to the servant role that Jesus adopts at the Last Supper when he washes the feet of his disciples (13:3-12).

Does the fact that John keeps the cross of Jesus before our eyes so insistently require us to revise the assertion with which we began this section? I do not think so. John neither glosses over the physical sufferings of Jesus nor does he dwell upon them for their own sake. For him, the passion of Jesus is also his glorification (12:23,27-28; cf. 13:31-32; 17:1,4-5). In it the saving mystery of the God of faithful love is revealed more clearly and more efficaciously than ever before in human history. Even (or should we say especially?) on the cross, Jesus' words to Philip ring true: 'Whoever has seen me has seen the Father' (14:9).

To help us to comprehend how the 'lifting up' of Jesus on a gibbet of shame could, in any sense, be an 'uplifting' event, let us consider two ways in which we use the word 'passion'. From the Latin *patior* (= to suffer or to endure), it is commonly employed in Christian theology to identify the sufferings and death of Jesus on the cross. However, the word 'passion' can also denote intense feeling or emotion, often deriving from or pointing to some deep commitment. It is probably not an oversimplification to suggest that the Johannine emphasis falls on the latter usage rather than on the former.

John consistently highlights the **voluntary** character of Jesus' sufferings (10:11,15,17-18; cf. 15:13). He presents Jesus as a prophetic figure who has good reason to believe that his uncompromising commitment to his Father's will (4:34; 5:19,30; cf. 8:28; 12:49-50; 14:10; 15:15) and unyielding fidelity to the mission entrusted to him will lead to his death. Eventually, he does die violently; and, as is the case with all true martyrs, Jesus' followers come to see his death as his moment of glory, redeemed from meaninglessness by the authenticity of the commitment to life that informed it. With the wisdom of hindsight his disciples could affirm that the light of the God-Man's love, experienced daily throughout his ministry among them, shone even more radiantly in the loveless darkness of sin which occasioned his death.

We can further enhance our understanding of the special quality of the Johannine passion narrative by noting both the details from the Synoptic accounts of the passion and death of Jesus that John chooses to omit and the details which are peculiar to his Gospel. Though these omissions and inclusions will be pointed out later at appropriate places in the commentary on John 18-19, it may be helpful to summarise them here. If it serves no other purpose, this should assist the reader to hear the whole passion narrative of the Fourth Gospel in the 'key' of John.

The following incidents, which are reported by at least two of the other Gospels, are **omitted by John:**

- the agony of Jesus in the garden (it is alluded to in 12:27-30; 18:11);

- the kiss whereby Judas, the betrayer, identifies Jesus;

- the desertion of Jesus by his disciples (he did foretell it, however, in 16:32);

- the full trial of Jesus before the Sanhedrin (it is hardly necessary in view of 11:47-53);

- the cruel mockery of Jesus as a prophet by the Roman soldiers;

- the incident involving the passer-by, Simon of Cyrene;

- the abusive remarks directed at Jesus on the cross;

- the anguished prayer of Jesus, 'My God, my God, why have you forsaken me?', and his loud cry as he expires;

- the menacing darkness that descends upon Calvary;

- the rending of the Temple curtain from top to bottom;

- the Roman centurion's public profession of faith.

The following details are **exclusively Johannine:**

- the involvement of a detachment of Roman soldiers in the arrest of Jesus;

- Jesus' words of power to the soldiers in the garden, 'I am he';

- the interrogation of Jesus by the power-broker, Annas;

- the opening clash between the Jews and Pontius Pilate;

- Pilate's private interview with Jesus in the praetorium;

- Pilate's two statements to Jesus' accusers, 'Here is the man!' and 'Here is your king!';

- Pilate's refusal to alter the inscription on the cross;

- the presence of the beloved disciple and the mother of Jesus at the foot of the cross;

- Jesus' words 'I am thirsty' and 'It is finished';

- the piercing of Jesus' side with a lance and the flow of blood and water;

- the ministry of Nicodemus at the burial of Jesus.

Like a typical Shakespearean play, John's account of the passion and death of Jesus can be divided into five acts:

1. Jesus accepts the cup of suffering: his demonstration of power (18:1-11).

2. The interrogation of Jesus before Annas: Peter's triple denial (18:12-27).

3. The trial of Jesus before Pontius Pilate (18:28 — 19:16a).

4. The way of the cross: the crucifixion of Jesus (19:16b-37).

5. The burial of Jesus (19:38-42).

The material in the detailed commentary will be presented under these headings.

Praying the Johannine passion narrative

In the Dogmatic Constitution on Divine Revelation (Flannery 1975:764) we are reminded that 'prayer should accompany the reading of sacred Scripture' (*Dei Verbum* 25). In similar vein St Augustine states that 'to understand Scripture, what is essential is to pray' (*De Doctrina Christiana*, 3, 37). Our prayer could take the form of *lectio divina* in which reflective reading of a chosen biblical text leads to contemplation; or, in the case of the chapters of John's Gospel we are considering, it could also find expression in traditional exercises of piety.

With these thoughts in mind, I have included after the commentary on John 18-19 a Way of the Cross based on the Fourth Gospel and a set of Johannine sorrowful mysteries of the Rosary.

Part 1

The Johannine passion narrative: a detailed commentary

1. Jesus accepts the cup of suffering: his demonstration of power (18:1-11)

18:1 After Jesus had spoken these words, he went out with his disciples across the Kidron valley to a place where there was a garden, which he and his disciples entered.

At the conclusion of the farewell discourse and his high priestly prayer, Jesus and his disciples set out across the Kidron valley and head towards a garden lying to the east of the city in the general direction of Bethany. It is a cold evening in early April; and, as it is Passover time, the moon is full.

On the way, they observe the shadowy outline of a number of familiar monuments ominously witnessing to the fact that this valley, the Valley of the King as it is also called, had been used in earlier times as a burial ground (2 Sam 18:18). It had also been associated with idolatrous rites which Asa (1 Kings 15:13), Hezekiah (2 Chron 29:10) and Josiah (2 Kings 23:4,6,12) had suppressed.

Awaiting Jesus, as he must surely know, is the same fate with which Solomon threatened Shimei: 'Build yourself a house in Jerusalem, and live there, and do not go out from there to any place whatever. For on the day you go out, and cross the Wadi Kidron, know for certain that you shall die ... ' (1 Kings 2:36-37).

John is the only one of the four evangelists who identifies the Kidron valley by name, thereby exploiting the dramatic potential of the associations that attach to that place. Moreover, while the other writers speak of Jesus' destination as the 'Mount of Olives' (Mt 26:30 // Mk 14:26 // Lk 22:39), he alone mentions the fact that there was a 'garden' there. Given John's penchant for symbolism, there may be an allusion here to the 'garden in Eden' (Gen 2:8-9) where Adam and Eve fell prey to the tempter's wiles. This interpretation is bolstered by the fact that only in the Fourth Gospel is it stated that the burial of Jesus takes place in a garden (19:41).

Just as the first Adam encountered the evil one in the form of a serpent (Gen 3), so also does Jesus, the new Adam, confront his great adversary in the person of the Iscariot — that one into whom Satan has entered (Jn 13:2,27; cf. 6:70; Lk 22:3).

Significantly, John does not follow the lead of Matthew (26:36) and Mark (14:32) in assigning the name 'Gethsemane' to the scene of Jesus' arrest. The omission is interesting in view of the fact that he is careful to preserve the names of

23

several other places connected with the passion of Jesus (cf. 19:13,17). Could it be that 'Gethsemane', an Aramaic word which denotes an oil press, has overtones that he finds jarring?

John's readers are invited to think of the garden primarily as a place where Jesus often entered into intimate communion with his own (18:2; cf. Lk 22:39). It is not intended to evoke memories of the bitter agony that Jesus endured there, crushed beneath the burden of his own anguish and our sin.

18:2 *Now Judas, who betrayed him, also knew the place, because Jesus often met there with his disciples.*

John, who develops the portrait of Judas more fully than the Synoptic writers do, reminds us repeatedly that the Iscariot's son is Jesus' betrayer (see also 6:71; 12:4; 13:21; 18:5).

From past experience (and possibly from arrangements made before or during the supper) Judas knows where to find Jesus and the other disciples. It is sadly ironic that his treacherous mission finishes in the very place where Jesus has shared his deepest thoughts with him.

Obviously, Jesus is no longer at pains to elude capture; for he knows that Judas will look for him here. His hour has come (cf. 13:1).

18:3 So Judas brought a detachment of soldiers together with police from the chief priests and the Pharisees, and they came there with lanterns and torches and weapons.

Many people lead others to Jesus in John's Gospel; indeed, this is one of the marks of the true disciple. The Baptist sends two of his own disciples to Jesus (1:35-37); Andrew, one of them, invites his brother Peter to meet 'the Messiah' (1:40-42); and Philip brings first Nathanael (1:45-46) and later 'some Greeks' (12:20-23) to Jesus. Especially noteworthy in this connection is the Samaritan woman who leads the towns-people of Sychar into the Lord's presence (4:5, 28-30).

However, whereas others bring their friends, Judas brings Jesus' enemies. In all four Gospel accounts of the apprehension of Jesus he is the guide (cf. Mt 26:47 // Mk 14:43 // Lk 22:47). Perhaps Judas is responding to the orders given by the chief priests and the Pharisees who had made it known 'that anyone who knew where Jesus was should let them know, so that they might arrest him' (11:57).[1]

---

1 Though the Pharisees are bracketed with the chief priests in 18:3, they are not mentioned again by the evangelist. Despite their apparent power in John's account of the cure of the man born blind (9:1-41), they were not the dominant force in Jesus' day that

Accompanying Judas is a detachment of Roman soldiers (a detail peculiar to John) and some temple police (cf. Lk 22:52).[2] Although the Greek original speaks of a 'cohort' of soldiers (600 men, one-tenth of a legion), it is more likely that the group numbered about 200 (that is, a maniple). Even so, the number may appear to be unduly large, given the task at hand; but we need to remember that the threat of disturbance to the established order was greater than usual when the Jewish people were celebrating the great feast of their liberation. However, the enthusiastic welcome accorded to Jesus as he entered the city of Jerusalem (12:12-19) cannot have escaped the notice of the Roman authorities.

Ranged against Jesus, as McHugh (1982:119) expresses it, is 'triple alliance of opponents: a

they were to become by the time of the writing of the Fourth Gospel (that is, after the destruction of the Temple in 70 C.E.). Moreover, the Synoptic writers do not mention the Pharisees at all in the course of their passion narratives. Like John, as a perusal of these narratives would clearly indicate, they attach greater importance to the role played by the chief priests. Indeed, Luke speaks of the priests not only as sending people to arrest Jesus (cf. Mt 26:47 // Mk 14:43) but as members of the group who actually do so (Lk 22:52).

2 Without implicating the Romans, Mark and Luke note the presence of 'a crowd' and Matthew refers to 'a great crowd' (Mt 26:47 // Mk 14:43 // Lk 22:47). For his part, John makes no reference to the people generally either in the arrest of Jesus or in the trial before Pilate.

renegade Christian, Roman troops, and Jewish police'.

The reference to 'lanterns and torches', which serves to emphasise the surrounding darkness, is a distinctively Johannine touch. If it is symbolic, it is also ironic in view of the fact that Jesus' captors stand before the one who has declared himself to be 'the light of the world' (8:12; cf. 1:4-5,9; 3:19; 12:46). It is truly '[their] hour, and the power of darkness!' (Lk 22:53).

18:4 Then Jesus, knowing all that was to happen to him, came forward and asked them, 'Whom are you looking for?'

Even though Judas figures more prominently in the Fourth Gospel than in the Synoptic writings, there is no reference to his kissing Jesus (cf. Mt 26:49//Mk 14:45//Lk 22:47). There is no need for this sign; for the Jesus of John's Gospel is always in control of the situation — an insight which the Divine Liturgy of St John Chrysostom captures when it speaks of 'the night he was delivered up or rather delivered himself up'. As we shall soon see, it is not Jesus but his enemies who are powerless in this encounter.

In his 'good shepherd' discourse Jesus had said, 'No one takes [my life] from me, but I lay it down of my own accord. I have power to lay

27

it down, and I have power to take it up again'
(10:18). Consistent with that assertion and like
one who has already 'conquered the world'
(16:33), Jesus himself takes the initiative; and,
stepping forward voluntarily to meet his foes, he
asks them, 'Whom are you looking for?'

The question is reminiscent of his first recorded words in the Gospel, spoken to the two disciples of the Baptist (1:38). It is the same question
he puts to the grieving Magdalen on Easter
morning (20:15).

*18:5 They answered, 'Jesus of Nazareth.' Jesus
replied, 'I am he.' Judas, who betrayed him, was
standing with them.*

John identifies the Saviour by his place of
origin (cf. 19:19 — the inscription on the cross)
as if to stress his humble origins and to suggest
that something good can come out of Nazareth
(cf. 1:46).

In replying to the soldiers, 'I am he' (Gk *ego
eimi*), Jesus makes use of the divine 'name' (cf.
Ex 3:14)[3], thereby implying equality with God.

---

3 This is clearer in the New American Bible which translates Jesus'
  reply in 18:5 simply as 'I AM'. The same version renders God's
  words to Moses in Ex 3:14 as follows: 'I am who am.' ... 'This
  is what you shall tell the Israelites: I AM sent me to you.' Out
  of reverence for the divine name, the term 'Adonai' (= my Lord)

Not for nothing will his opponents accuse him of blasphemy (Jn 19:7; cf. Mt 26:65 // Mk 14:64).

> *18:6 When Jesus said to them, 'I am he,' they stepped back and fell to the ground.*

The reaction of Jesus' enemies is in keeping with the fear which is usually felt by recipients of heavenly visitations in the Sacred Scriptures (cf. Mt 28:4-5,8; Lk 2:9; Mk 16:5-6,8; etc.). However, with reference to the Roman soldiers, who presumably do not know that Jesus has uttered the divine name (cf. 13:18-19), we may assume that their fear stems from the commanding presence and the extraordinary composure of Jesus. Their sentiments echo those of the temple police who, having aborted a previous mission to arrest him, remarked: 'Never has anyone spoken like this!' (7:46).

John's readers might well have recalled the words of the Psalmist[4] (Ps 27:2; cf. Ps 9:3; 35:4; 56:9; Is 11:4):

---

was used instead in public reading of the Hebrew Scriptures. Other pertinent texts in the Fourth Gospel include 8:24,28,58.

4 Note that, in numbering the psalms, the NRSV (like the NJB and the NAB) follows the Hebrew system of numbering. From Ps 10 to Ps 147 this is ahead of the Gk and Vulgate system which is followed in some translations. Moreover, the numbering of the verses in the NAB is usually one behind that given in the NRSV and the NJB.

When evil doers assail me
to devour my flesh —
my adversaries and foes —
they shall stumble and fall.

They may have called to mind also the fate of the successive groups of soldiers sent by King Ahaziah to Elijah the Tishbite (2 Kings 1:9-14).

18:7 Again he asked them, 'Whom are you looking for?' And they said, 'Jesus of Nazareth.' 8 Jesus answered, 'I told you that I am he. So if you are looking for me, let these men go.'

It is interesting that the only person who gives orders during the arrest of Jesus is not, as one might expect, the officer of the Roman soldiers but Jesus himself who 'shows himself mighty against his foes' (Is 42:13).

Note, too, the solicitude of Jesus for his disciples; he is indeed the good shepherd caring for his own so that 'the evil one does not touch them' (1 Jn 5:18). They do not flee in disarray as they do in the Synoptic Gospels although Jesus had foretold during the Last Supper that they would (16:32).

18:9 This was to fulfill the word that he had spoken, 'I did not lose a single one of those whom you gave me.'

Asides are a feature of the Fourth Gospel. This one recalls Jesus' words in the 'bread of life' discourse: 'And this is the will of him who sent me, that I should lose nothing of all that he has given me, but raise it up on the last day' (6:39; cf. 10:28; 17:12).

> **18:10** *Then Simon Peter, who had a sword, drew it, struck the high priest's slave, and cut off his right ear. The slave's name was Malchus.*

John's Gospel is in accord with that of Luke (22:50,54) in placing this rather vicious intervention on the part of one of the disciples before the actual seizure of Jesus. Matthew (26:50-51) and Mark (14:46-47), on the other hand, choose to include it after Jesus is apprehended.

Though all the evangelists would doubtless agree that such rash and impetuous behaviour is in character for Peter, only John mentions him by name as the assailant. Likewise he alone records the name of Malchus, the uncomprehending disciple's victim. Peter comes close on this occasion to making good his boast to Jesus, 'I will lay down my life for you' (13:37).

Unlike Luke, who also observes that it is the servant's right ear which is severed (Lk 22:50), John sees no good reason to interrupt the flow of his narrative by including Jesus' healing of the wounded man (cf. Lk 22:51).

18:11 Jesus said to Peter, 'Put your sword back into its sheath. Am I not to drink the cup that the Father has given me?'

On four occasions the Jews had tried unsuccessfully to arrest Jesus (7:30,44; 8:20; 10:39); and more than once he had found it necessary to hide from them (8:59; 12:36). However, knowing that his hour has now come, Jesus deliberately refrains from evasive action; and, as he makes clear to Peter, he has no need of the services of a bodyguard (cf. 18:36).

Matthew has Jesus give Peter some practical advice, 'Put your sword back into its place; for all who take the sword will perish by the sword' (Mt 26:52; cf. Lk 22:51). Not surprisingly, John gives a more 'theological' reason for not resorting to violence.

In Jesus' protestation, 'Am I not to drink the cup that the Father has given me?' (cf. Mt 26:39//Mk 14:35-36//Lk 22:41-42; Heb 5:7-10), we have an allusion (cf. 12:27) to the agony he endured in the garden — an episode which John, for reasons which should now be obvious, chooses to omit. With this dramatic question the evangelist brings to a close the introductory scene of his passion narrative.

2. The interrogation of Jesus before Annas: Peter's triple denial (18:12-27)

18:12 So the soldiers, their officer, and the Jewish police arrested Jesus and bound him.

On a previous occasion, during the Jewish festival of Booths (7:2), the Pharisees had sent the temple police to arrest Jesus but they had returned with their mission unfulfilled saying, 'Never has anyone spoken like this!' (7:32,45-46). 'No one arrested him', we read a little later in the text, 'because his hour had not yet come' (8:20).

This time, however, things are different; Jesus is fully aware that the long awaited hour has come for him 'to depart from this world and go to the Father' (13:1). Offering no resistance, he permits the temple police with the aid of the Roman soldiers to apprehend him and bind him. How ironic it is that they should bind the one who is the source of all true human freedom and its prime exemplar.

For some readers the binding of Jesus, who will later carry the wood of the cross up the mountain of sacrifice, may be evocative of the image of Isaac in the Hebrew Scriptures (cf. Gen 22:6,9).

18:13 First they took him to Annas, who was the father-in-law of Caiaphas, the high priest that year.

There is no appearance of Jesus before the Sanhedrin in John's Gospel. The record of such an interrogation would add little to what we already know about the authorities' attitude to Jesus and about their intentions to get him out of the way (cf. 7:45-52; 11:45-54). Jesus has already been condemned *in absentia* by Caiaphas in his unconsciously ironic words to the Sanhedrin after the raising of Lazarus: 'You know nothing at all! You do not understand that it is better for you to have one man die for the people than to have the whole nation destroyed' (11:49-50).

In the Synoptic writings there is no mention of Jesus' appearance before Annas; he is taken directly to Caiaphas (cf. Mt 26:57 // Mk 14:53 // Lk 22:54). Perhaps John is suggesting that Annas, who was high priest between 6 and 15 C.E. until he was deposed by Pilate's predecessor, is still the power behind the throne (cf. Lk 3:2; Acts 4:6). He and several of his sons in succession exercised the high priestly office in ways which did not endear them to the Jewish people.

18:14 Caiaphas was the one who had advised the Jews that it was better to have one person die for the people.

Cross-referencing of this kind is a feature of the Fourth Gospel; it contributes in a small way to the overall unity of the work. The irony of Caiaphas's remark lies in the fact that Jesus does in fact die for all people, Caiaphas included.

18:15 Simon Peter and another disciple followed Jesus. Since that disciple was known to the high priest, he went with Jesus into the courtyard of the high priest, ...

Since there is no reference to Jesus' being sent to Caiaphas until 18:24, it could be that the 'high priest' referred to in this verse is Annas himself. This is not altogether surprising; for there are precedents for a person's retaining a title in an honorific way even after he or she has left office (cf. Lk 3:2; Acts 4:6). Another possibility is that the interrogation before Annas actually takes place at the home of his son-in-law.

With new-found courage, Simon Peter (John frequently speaks of him in this way) in company with another disciple of Jesus makes his way to the high priest's courtyard. In the Synoptic accounts he is unaccompanied (Mt 26:58 // Mk 14:54 // Lk 22:54). Given the fact that Peter and the beloved disciple are linked elsewhere in the Gospel (20:2,4; 21:20-23), it is a reasonable assumption that it is this disciple, unique to the Fourth Gospel, who is Peter's unnamed companion.

We need not read too much into the phrase, 'known to the high priest'; it may indicate nothing more than a friendly relationship with members of the high priest's household.

> *18:16 ... but Peter was standing outside at the gate. So the other disciple, who was known to the high priest, went out, spoke to the woman who guarded the gate, and brought Peter in.*

The repeated use of the word 'disciple' in 18:15-27, serves to highlight the infidelity of Peter. His conduct, as we shall see in the following verses, is unworthy of a follower of Jesus.

When we consider the size of the detachment sent to arrest Jesus, it is rather surprising to find a woman guarding the gate.

> *18:17 The woman said to Peter, 'You are not also one of this man's disciples, are you?' He said, 'I am not.'*

There is a marked contrast between the weakness of Peter on this occasion and the strength which Jesus consistently displays. Set against Jesus' resolute 'I am' in the garden, Peter's 'I am not' is a less than courageous response to the woman's question and is quite unworthy of a disciple.

We may discern a pastoral relevance in John's recounting of these events. He would have his community follow the example of Jesus and not that of Peter in their confrontations with the Jewish authorities. 'You are not also one of this man's disciples, are you?' is a question that had been frequently put to them in the years following the death and resurrection of Jesus.

18:18 Now the slaves and the police had made a charcoal fire because it was cold, and they were standing around it and warming themselves. Peter also was standing with them and warming himself.

As Jerusalem is elevated, it is not unusual for the evenings to be cold in early April. Both Mark and Luke also remark that there is a fire in the courtyard (see Mk 14:54 // Lk 22:55). However, John's observation that it is a 'charcoal' fire suggests an eye-witness account and adds a note of verisimilitude to the text. This is an important detail because it links Peter's threefold denial of Jesus with his later triple protestation of love for him which will also take place before a 'charcoal fire' (21:9,15-19).

18:19 Then the high priest questioned Jesus about his disciples and about his teaching.

By directing our attention to the high priest's interrogation of Jesus at this point, John, unlike the Synoptic writers (cf. Mt 26:69-74 // Mk 14:66-72 // Lk 22:55-60), breaks up the three denials of Peter. This placement of Peter's denials on either side of Jesus' resolute stand before the high priest reinforces the contrast between the two men on trial and thereby adds to the dramatic effect of the narrative.

It is interesting to note that Annas, in this preliminary hearing, questions Jesus first about his disciples. Though Jesus is known to be opposed to violence, it could well be that the high priest fears that his prisoner could, nonetheless, be the inspiration of a popular uprising and the indirect cause of bloody intervention on the part of the Romans (cf. 11:48). He has grounds for such fear; for Pilate was a brute who, according to Josephus Flavius, had once crucified 3000 Galileans after a riot.

> **18:20** *Jesus answered, 'I have spoken openly to the world; I have always taught in the synagogues and in the temple, where all the Jews come together. I have said nothing in secret.*

Safeguarding their interests, Jesus makes no response concerning his disciples; but he willingly speaks to Annas about his teaching in the synagogue (cf. 6:59) and in the Temple (cf. 7:14,28; 8:20; 10:23) — the preferred places (in the Fourth Gospel) in which he had exercised his preaching ministry.

Jesus' statement that he has always spoken publicly is similar to his protestation in the

Synoptic Gospels at the time of his apprehension: 'Day after day I sat in the temple teaching, and you did not arrest me' (Mt 26:55 // Mk 14:49 // Lk 22:53; cf. Is 45:19; 48:16).

18:21 Why do you ask me? Ask those who heard what I said to them; they know what I said.'

It is quite improper under rabbinic law to seek a conviction by requiring an accused person to testify against himself. Rightly, therefore, does Jesus invite Annas to call as witnesses for the defence those who had heard him speak. Truth to tell, their understanding of his teaching was often very limited.

This scene is reminiscent of earlier controversies in the Gospel (cf. 7:25-39; 8:25-26; 9 *passim*; 10:22-39) which is pervaded by a trial atmosphere.

18:22 When he had said this, one of the police standing nearby struck Jesus on the face, saying, 'Is that how you answer the high priest?'

All the Gospels report the verbal and physical abuse to which Jesus is subjected. However, John's account is both milder and more economical in this regard. Though he alone records this incident, he omits altogether the gross maltreatment of Jesus at the hands of the Roman soldiers (cf. Mt 26:67-68 // Mk 14:65 // Lk 22:63-65; and

Mt 27:27-31 // Mk 15:16-20) and the abuse of Jesus on the cross (cf. Mt 27:39-44 // Mk 15: 29-32 // Lk 23:35-39). Such humiliation is out of place in what is, for John, the moment of Jesus' exaltation when his glory is revealed.

The action of the sychophantic policeman in striking Jesus, who like the Isaian suffering servant does not defend himself (cf. Is 50:6), compounds the injustice of the situation.

18:23 Jesus answered, 'If I have spoken wrongly, testify to the wrong. But if I have spoken rightly, why do you strike me?'

Jesus, who is always in control of the situation in John's Gospel, continues to give an object lesson on how Christians should behave in the face of persecution. His dignity is enhanced by his composure in the face of physical abuse. For an interesting parallel, read the account of Paul's trial before the high priest Ananias (Acts 23:1-5).

Jesus' response to the man who assaulted him recalls his words to the Jews during an earlier altercation: 'Which of you convicts me of sin? If I tell the truth, why do you not believe me?' (8:46).

18:24 Then Annas sent him bound to Caiaphas the high priest.

Unlike the other evangelists (Mt 26:57-75 // Mk 14:53-72 // Lk 22:54-71) John does not give any details of the trial before 'Caiaphas the high priest, in whose house the scribes and the elders had gathered' (Mt 26:57). He merely notes that Annas sends him bound to his son-in-law. It will serve John's theological purpose more adequately to develop at greater length than the Synoptic writers do the trial before Pilate.

We have in this verse the second of three references to Jesus' being bound (cf. 18:12). The final one is to the burial garments which, in contrast to those of Lazarus (11:44), Jesus leaves behind in the tomb on the morning of his resurrection from the dead (19:40).

> *18:25 Now Simon Peter was standing and warming himself. They asked him, 'You are not also one of his disciples, are you?' He denied it and said, 'I am not.'*

It could well be that Peter's second denial is uttered in the hearing of Jesus as he is being led away through the courtyard (cf. Lk 22:61). One might argue that Peter is speaking the truth because by now he has forfeited any claim to being Jesus' disciple. However, let us not be too hard on him; at least, Peter is there. Where are the others?

Keeping his focus always on Jesus, John does not record the grief of Peter (cf. Mt 26:75 // Mk 14:72 // Lk 22:62) who must surely have been the more upset in view of his boast that he would die for Jesus if put to the test. 'Lord, why can I not follow you now? I will lay down my life for you', he had said after the washing of the feet (13:37).

There will be time later by the shore of the lake for him to express his repentance and to receive the love and forgiveness of Jesus Risen (21:15-19). John's perspective is theological, not psychological.

18:26 One of the slaves of the high priest, a relative of the man whose ear Peter had cut off, asked, 'Did I not see you in the garden with him?'

Peter is under suspicion not because of his Galilean accent (cf. Mt 26:73 // Mk 14:70 // Lk 22:59) but because he is recognised as the man who wounded Malchus in the garden (18:10).

18:27 Again Peter denied it, and at that moment the cock crowed.

In the Fourth Gospel Peter does not deny Jesus with an oath or invoke a curse upon himself (cf. Mt 26:72,74; Mk 14:71). There is something perhaps even more pathetic in the matter of fact way in which his 'rejection' of Jesus is recorded.

Jesus' prophecy has been fulfilled: 'Will you lay down your life for me? Very truly, I tell you, before the cock crows, you will have denied me three times' (13:38).

3. The trial of Jesus before Pontius Pilate (18:28—19:16a)

18:28 Then they took Jesus from Caiaphas to Pilate's headquarters. It was early in the morning. They themselves did not enter the headquarters, so as to avoid ritual defilement and to be able to eat the Passover.

It was night when Judas left the supper room on his mission of betrayal (13:30) and when Jesus was arrested in the garden across the Kidron valley (cf. 18:3). Now, in Bultmann's (1971:651) words, 'The day of the victory of Jesus over the world is breaking.' He is taken, presumably by a detail of Roman soldiers, to the headquarters ('praetorium' in the Greek text) of Pontius Pilate who was the Roman prefect of Judea between 26 and 36 C.E.

The location of the praetorium is debated by scholars. For most of the year, the prefect (or the 'governor' as he is referred to in the New Testament) lived in more salubrious surroundings at Caesarea on the coast (cf. Acts 23:33), moving to Jerusalem at certain times, like Passover, when patriotic feeling ran high among the people. On such occasions one might expect to find additional soldiers stationed at the Fortress Antonia overlooking the Temple.

The fact that the Jewish authorities refuse to enter Pilate's headquarters enables the writer to use to excellent dramatic effect the two stage technique. Compare the Synoptic accounts where all the participants in the trial are gathered in the one place (Mt 27:11-14 // Mk 15:2-5 // Lk 23:2-5; and Mt 27:15-26 // Mk 15:6-15 // Lk 23: 17-25).

How ironical it is that these Jews should wish to remain ritually clean for the eating of the Passover meal when the very 'Lamb of God' (1:29, 36) is about to be delivered over to death by them. Unwittingly, as Brown (1970:866) points out, 'they are making possible the true Passover.'

Actually, it is arguable whether or not they would have been defiled on this occasion by entering the praetorium; but their reluctance is understandable. Recall Peter's words to the household of Cornelius: 'You yourselves know that it is unlawful for a Jew to associate with or to visit a Gentile; but God has shown me that I should not call anyone profane or unclean' (Acts 10:28).

From the concern expressed by Jesus' accusers, we may conclude that the trial and the crucifixion take place a day earlier in John than in the Synoptic narratives. This need not disturb us unduly if we keep in mind that historical detail, though it is obviously important, is always subservient to theological intent in the Gospels.

18:29 So Pilate went out to them and said, 'What accusation do you bring against this man?'

It is hardly likely that a Roman tribune would have carried out the arrest of Jesus, in collaboration with Jewish police, without the knowledge of the prefect. Pilate's question to the Jews is not intended to dispel ignorance on his part but to initiate the trial proceedings in a formal manner.

18:30 They answered, 'If this man were not a criminal, we would not have handed him over to you.'

Evasive rather than insolent, Jesus' enemies are reluctant to declare their hand at this stage. They do not immediately lay the three specific charges we find in the Lucan account: 'We found this man perverting our nation, forbidding us to pay taxes to the emperor, and saying that he himself is the Messiah, a king' (Lk 23:2).

However, they make their intentions abundantly clear in the following verse.

45

18:31 Pilate said to them, 'Take him yourselves and judge him according to your law.' The Jews replied, 'We are not permitted to put anyone to death.'

There is a measure of irony in the Jewish leaders'[5] response to Pilate's sarcastic suggestion that they should judge Jesus according to their own law; they have been doing so for some time with embarrassing results for themselves.

The Romans denied conquered peoples the right to put anyone to death (the *ius gladii*) without their approval. Whereas they resorted to the barbarity of crucifixion, stoning was the common method of execution employed by the Jews for such heinous crimes as idolatry (Deut 13:6-11; 17:2-7), blasphemy (Lev 24:14-16,23), profaning the sabbath (Num 15:35,36), stubborn rebellion against one's parents (Deut 21:18-21) and fornication (Deut 22:20-21). Note also

---

5 In 18:31 and in 70 other places in his Gospel, John speaks of 'the Jews' (Gk *hoi Ioudaioi*). Unfortunately, as the expression frequently has a negative connotation for him, the evangelist has apparently left himself open to the accusation of anti-Semitism. This difficulty would be overcome and the writer's intentions would be better respected if translations made it clear when *hoi Ioudaioi* referred to the people as a whole, to the Judeans, or (as in this and other polemical passages) to the religious authorities in Jerusalem. John is not antipathetic towards the Jewish people. He acknowledges the Jewishness of Jesus (cf. 18:35) and records Jesus' words to the Samaritan woman that 'salvation is from the Jews' (4:22).

Jn 8:4-5 — the woman taken in adultery; and Acts 7:54-60 — Stephen.

In any case, in view of the growing support for Jesus among the people (cf 12:12-13,20-21, 42), his opponents think that crucifixion by the Romans is the better course of action.

18:32 (This was to fulfil what Jesus had said when he indicated the kind of death he was to die.)

This verse, one of many 'asides' in the Fourth Gospel, repeats almost word for word the evangelist's interpretation in 12:33 of the prophecy that Jesus made soon after his triumphal entry into Jerusalem, namely that he would be 'lifted up from the earth' (12:32; cf. 3:14; 8:28) and thus 'draw all people to [himself]'. Duke (1985:129) remarks perceptively:

> *By pointing to this previous prediction, the author indirectly presents the larger irony of the Gospel. 'The Jews' have him shamefully crucified to prevent the world from going after him, when in fact he long ago had chosen just such a way to gather the world unto himself.*

18:33 Then Pilate entered the headquarters again, summoned Jesus, and asked him, 'Are you the King of the Jews?'

The fact that this is Pilate's first question to Jesus in all four Gospels (cf. Mt 27:11 // Mk

15:2 // Lk 23:3) would seem to indicate that we are here in touch with the earliest tradition. Pilate gets straight to the point; he does not share Annas's interest in Jesus' teaching. His question, prompted perhaps by some report he has heard, is a purely political one for a Roman even though it would have had religious significance as well for a Jew. It is about power and, therefore, about a possible threat to his authority.

Earlier in the Gospel Jesus had been addressed as 'King' (1:49; 12:13); but, as with all the titles accorded him, Jesus is concerned to purify it of any political or nationalistic overtones. In truth, Pilate has nothing to fear on this score.

In view of the fact that there are no fewer than twelve references to Jesus' kingship in the Johannine passion story, it is not without good reason that Forestell (1974:83) observes: 'The kingship of Jesus is clearly the principal theme of the passion narrative in the fourth gospel.'

18:34 Jesus answered, 'Do you ask this on your own, or did others tell you about me?'

We may note in passing that the dialogue in this section is typically Johannine and probably has its reflex in the daily life of the writer's community.

Jesus' response to Pilate is fuller in John than in the Synoptic Gospels (cf. Mt 27:11 // Mk 15:2 // Lk 23:3). He, in his turn, confronts Pilate with a question regarding the source of his information. Implicit in this enquiry of Jesus is another question, 'Are you speaking from a Roman understanding of a king or from a Jewish understanding?' Without this necessary clarification, Jesus cannot hope to share his own self-awareness with the Roman prefect.

> *18:35 Pilate replied, 'I am not a Jew, am I? Your own nation and the chief priests have handed you over to me. What have you done?'*

Having received no satisfactory answer from Jesus' accusers concerning his captive's misdemeanours (18:29-30), Pilate now asks Jesus himself, 'What have you done?' But just as the Roman refrained from answering Jesus' question, so Jesus does not respond directly to this new query. If he were disposed to do so, he could well repeat what he said to 'the Jews' on another occasion when his life was under threat: 'I have shown you many good works from the Father. For which of these are you going to stone me?' (10:32; cf. 5:36).

Contemptuous of the Jews in general, Pilate seems to be impressed as the trial proceeds by the demeanour of Jesus. He is even vaguely afraid of him (cf. 19:8).

18:36 Jesus answered, 'My kingdom is not from this world. If my kingdom were from this world, my followers would be fighting to keep me from being handed over to the Jews. But as it is, my kingdom is not from here.'

Jesus makes it clear to Pilate that he is not a menace to the Romans; for his kingship has little in common with the popular Jewish concept of the Messiah. He had repulsed the attempt of the Galileans to make him a king in the political sense (6:15); and he had entered Jerusalem for the celebration of the Passover feast not as a symbol of revolutionary power but humbly on the back of a donkey (12:14-16; cf. Zech 9:9).

Earthly kings have bodyguards; but Jesus has already demonstrated in the garden that he has no need for sword-wielding protectors (18:11).

Even after his resurrection Jesus' disciples do not fully grasp the true nature of his kingship. 'Lord, is this the time', they ask him, 'when you will restore the kingdom to Israel?' (Acts 1:6; cf. Lk 24:21).

18:37 Pilate asked him, 'So you are a king?' Jesus answered, 'You say that I am a king. For this I was born, and for this I came into the world, to testify

*to the truth. Everyone who belongs to the truth
listens to my voice.'*

Jesus accepts the title of king but not the concept, Roman or Jewish. In this somewhat reluctant affirmation of his kingly status, we have one of the key texts for understanding the nature of Jesus' mission (cf. 3:16; 10:10; 12:46).

Truth is one of the important themes of John's Gospel. To know the truth which Jesus, the one who is 'full of grace and truth' (1:14; cf. 1:17), has come to reveal is to have insight into the divine scheme of things. This is what Jesus had tried to convey previously to those plotting his death when he said, 'If you were Abraham's children, you would be doing what Abraham did, but now you are trying to kill me, a man who has told you the truth that I heard from God' (8:39-40). Read 8:39-47; cf. 3:31-36.

In speaking of himself as the good shepherd Jesus had said: 'I have other sheep that do not belong to this fold. I must bring them also, and they will listen to my voice' (10:16; cf. 10:3,27). Unfortunately, Pilate, who is one of these 'other sheep', does not listen to Jesus' voice and can manage only a bumbling (or is it cynical?) retort.

*18:38 Pilate asked him, 'What is truth?'
After he had said this, he went out to the Jews again
and told them, 'I find no case against him …'*

51

What a consummate ironist the writer of this Gospel is! The answer to Pilate's question (if indeed it is a question) is standing before him in the person of Jesus who had said of himself, 'I am the truth' (14:6). The word 'truth' is not used in the remainder of the Gospel.

Pilate goes out to the Jewish authorities again at this point and for the first of three times (cf. 19:4,6) proclaims the innocence of Jesus. In this movement to and fro between Jesus and those gathered outside the praetorium, we have an image of the vacillation of his mind as he seeks not so much justice for Jesus as freedom from harassment for himself. Brown (1986:60) captures this indecision well when he writes: 'As he moves from one stage to the other, Pilate is like a chameleon, taking on the different coloration of the parties who engage him.'

Luke is the only other Gospel writer who draws our attention to the Roman's declaration of Jesus' innocence; and, as in the Johannine account, it is mentioned three times (Lk 23:4, 14,22).

18:39 '... But you have a custom that I release someone for you at the Passover. Do you want me to release for you the King of the Jews?'

Pilate now makes a tactical error, based on an unwarranted assumption, which recalls the folly of Herod's promise to Salome (Mt 14:7 // Mk 6:23). He proposes to release Jesus in keeping with the terms of a Passover amnesty.

We may note in passing that, although all four evangelists refer to this amnesty (cf. Mt 27: 15-21 // Mk 15:6-11 // Lk 23:17-19), there is no extra-biblical evidence for it.

John's account of the Barabbas incident has some affinities with that of Mark (for example, in the use of the phrase 'King of the Jews'); but John switches the initiative from the Jews to Pilate.

18:40 They shouted in reply, 'Not this man, but Barabbas!' Now Barabbas was a bandit.

The 'they', I believe, identifies the chief priests (cf. 19:15) and not a crowd of people who have been manipulated by them (as in Mt 27:20 // Mk 15:11)[6] into pressing for the release of Barabbas.

Barabbas (a patronymic meaning 'son of the father') is variously described in the Gospels as 'a notorious prisoner' (Mt 27:16), as 'a man ... in prison with the rebels who had committed murder during the insurrection' (Mk 15:7; cf.

---

6 Luke implicates 'crowds (23:4) and 'the people' (23:13); but he makes no reference to their being stirred up by the leaders.

Lk 23:19; Acts 3:14), and as a 'bandit' (Jn 18:40, translating the Greek word *lestes*). Because he is a more obvious political threat than Jesus, it is ironical that Pilate should let him go rather than the Nazarene.

As he avoids unnecessary detail which would distract our attention from Jesus, John does not mention the actual release of Barabbas (cf. Mt 27:26 // Mk 15:15 // Lk 23:24-25).

19:1 Then Pilate took Jesus and had him flogged.

In the two Synoptic Gospels which mention the scourging of Jesus, it takes place at the end of the Roman trial, immediately before the crucifixion (Mt 27:26 // Mk 15:15); but it suits John's dramatic and theological purpose to make it central to the trial scene itself. If nothing else, it will serve to heighten the tension when, a little later in the piece, a wounded Jesus is presented to his accusers (19:5) and all the significant players in the drama are brought together for the first time.

Considering Pilate's declaration of Jesus' innocence, the scourging highlights the injustice of the man. Is it perhaps an attempt to extract some kind of a confession from Jesus?

19:2 And the soldiers wove a crown of thorns and put it on his head, and they dressed him in a purple robe.

If you compare the scourging and crowning of Jesus in the various accounts (Luke characteristically omits these details), you will notice that John writes much more economically than Matthew and Mark (cf. Mt 27:27-31 // Mk 15:16-20). He sees no good reason for detailing the physical and verbal abuse to which Jesus is subjected.

In dressing Jesus up as a king, the Roman soldiers (possibly a rag-tag group of Syrian conscripts) may have been playing a version of the ancient game, *Basilicus*, in which 'homage' is accorded mockingly to someone, chosen by lot, who agrees to pay a forfeit in return for these signal 'favours'. In Jesus' case the crown of thorns is placed on his head in grotesque imitation of the laurel wreath with which Roman emperors were sometimes adorned.

Though the soldiers would not have been aware of the fact, we may note in passing that purple garments were worn by the kings of Midian (Judg 8:26).

19:3 They kept coming up to him, saying, 'Hail, King of the Jews!' and striking him on the face.

Both the irony and the pathos of this scene lie in the fact that Jesus is indeed what the soldiers mockingly call him — 'King of the Jews' (cf.

55

Mt 27:29 // Mk 15:18). He is their king in a way that Caesar can never be.

> *19:4 Pilate went out again and said to them, 'Look, I am bringing him out to you to let you know that I find no case against him.'*

How, we might ask, can Pilate possibly think that he can establish Jesus' innocence to the satisfaction of anyone (especially his enemies) after he has just had him scourged?

> *19:5 So Jesus came out, wearing the crown of thorns and the purple robe. Pilate said to them, 'Here is the man!'*

With Pilate at his side, the bruised and bloody Jesus, still wearing the crown of thorns and the purple robe (cf. Rev 19:13), is presented to his enemies. Whatever his appearance to the onlookers, he is a king for this evangelist. Significantly, the accounts in Matthew and Mark state that the cloak was removed immediately after the scourging (cf. Mt 27:31 // Mk 15:20).

Pilate's exclamation, 'Here is the man!' (cf. 19:14), is probably more sarcastic than compassionate, although it could be argued that he is endeavouring to arouse some measure of sympathy in the hearts of Jesus' enemies. He does not realise, of course, that 'the man' he displays to the Jewish leaders is no mere man but the very Son of God.

19:6 When the chief priests and the police saw him, they shouted, 'Crucify him! Crucify him!' Pilate said to them, 'Take him yourselves and crucify him; I find no case against him.'

In the cry of the chief priests and the police we have the first explicit mention of the cross in the passion narrative. The 'Hosannas!' which greeted the entry of 'the King of Israel' (12:12) into the city have given way to vociferous words of condemnation.

19:7 The Jews answered him, 'We have a law, and according to that law he ought to die because he has claimed to be the Son of God.'

At last Jesus' accusers declare their hand; he is a blasphemer (cf. 5:18; 10:33). They have waited until this moment to make their accusation, knowing that it would not have provided grounds for the death penalty under Roman law.

Understandably, Pilate would have been unmoved if they had sought to incriminate Jesus by quoting, at the beginning of their dialogue with him, relevant passages from the Hebrew Scriptures. 'One who blasphemes the name of the LORD shall be put to death; the whole congregation shall stone the blasphemer. Aliens as well as citizens, when they blaspheme the Name, shall be put to death' (Lev 24:16).

19:8 Now when Pilate heard this, he was more afraid than ever.

No reference has been made so far in the Gospel to fear on the part of Pilate. John does not record the anguished warning of Pilate's wife which would have given him good grounds for concern: 'Have nothing to do with that innocent man, for today I have suffered a great deal because of a dream about him' (Mt 27:19).

It could be that the expression 'Son of God' has aroused Pilate's superstitions. Could it be that this man of rare composure and strength who has stood unflinchingly before him is the son of a god?

19:9 He entered his headquarters again and asked Jesus, 'Where are you from?' But Jesus gave him no answer.

Pilate is not asking for Jesus' home address. His question might be rephrased, 'What is your mysterious origin?' It is a question which does not appear in the Synoptic Gospels; they do not dwell at length on the theme of Jesus' origin from the Father (cf. Jn 3:31-36; 6:32-40,50-51; 7:27-29; 8:14-16; 9:29,33; 16:25-28; 17:7,25-26).

For once Jesus does not reply. It is only the man or woman of faith who can appreciate the answer to any question that invites Jesus to reveal his identity (cf. 10:24-26). What answer can be given to a person who asks, 'What is truth?'

19:10 Pilate therefore said to him, 'Do you refuse to speak to me? Do you not know that I have power to release you, and power to crucify you?'

Despite the increasingly impatient Pilate's appeal to his authority as Roman prefect in Judea, the truth of the matter is that he has no ultimate power over Jesus. As Jesus has said, 'No one takes [my life] from me, but I lay it down of my own accord. I have power to lay it down, and I have power to take it up again' (10:18; cf. 14:30). Ironically and by way of contrast, Pilate is powerless before the will of the chief priests and their supporters.

19:11 Jesus answered him, 'You would have no power over me unless it had been given you from above; therefore the one who handed me over to you is guilty of a greater sin.'

Implicit in this response of Jesus is an answer to Pilate's question about his origins. Both he and Pilate derive whatever power they have from the same source. Legitimate authority, as distinct from political clout, comes from God (cf. Rom 13:1-3).

Those who have handed Jesus over to Pilate for judgment have the greater sin; for their rejection of him is not politically motivated, as it is with Pilate, but embodies a wilful failure to believe. This judgment calls to mind an observation which Jesus made during the supper discourse: 'If I had not come and spoken to them, they would not have sin; but now they have no excuse for their sin' (15:22).

Note that Jesus remains very much in control of the situation. In this connection, McHugh (1982:123) observes: 'Though the crowds may howl for his death, this bleeding prisoner is still capable of talking as an equal with the representative of Rome.'

> *19:12 From then on Pilate tried to release him, but the Jews cried out, 'If you release this man, you are no friend of the emperor. Everyone who claims to be a king sets himself against the emperor.'*

There is a somewhat awkward transition here, for we are not told that Pilate has gone outside. It is obvious, however, that he is confronting the hostile gathering once more. This time they endeavour to bring even greater pressure to bear on him by resorting to what can only be called blackmail. Implicit in their use of the honorific title 'friend of the emperor' (it was bestowed on those who had rendered him conspicuous service) is the suggestion that the emperor might become decidedly unfriendly towards Pilate if he tolerates rivals to Roman power like Jesus.

Evans (1977:61) describes the situation well when he observes:

> *The roles are now reversed. In place of the Roman governor offering the Jewish people the choice, "Which will you have, Jesus or Barabbas?" the Jewish people offer the governor the choice, "Which will you have, Christ or Caesar?"*

> *19:13 When Pilate heard these words, he brought Jesus outside and sat on the judge's bench at a place called The Stone Pavement, or in Hebrew Gabbatha.*

In a number of modern translations of this verse (for example, the *New Jerusalem Bible* and the revised (1986) *New American Bible*), it is Jesus and not Pilate who is seated on the judge's bench. This is a reading which an increasing number of scholars support. If this is the case, it could be an attempt on the part of Pilate to mock Jesus just as his soldiers did (19:2-3). In any event, it is appropriate because Jesus is the only true judge present (cf. 5:22; 9:39). Pilate does not in fact pass judgment on Jesus anywhere in the passion narrative.

Only John mentions the Hebrew (more correctly, Aramaic) equivalent of the Greek word

Lithostrotos ('The Stone Pavement'). 'Gabbatha' means a height or an eminence and is not, therefore, a direct translation. This is yet another example of the writer's considerable local knowledge (cf. 19:17).

19:14 Now it was the day of Preparation for the Passover; and it was about noon. He said to the Jews, 'Here is your King!'

The fact that John gives two time details and (in the previous verse) two place details in connection with this event of Jesus' 'coronation' indicates the importance that he attaches to it. It also lends weight, I believe, to the above suggestion that Jesus is the one seated on the judge's bench.

Pilate's statement, 'Here is your King!' (cf. 19:5), climaxes the kingship theme in the Gospel.

The Passover officially commenced at noon — the deadline for keeping leavened bread. At this time the slaughter of the Passover lambs began in preparation for the feast. It is precisely at this time, in John's account of the passion, that the fate of the true Passover lamb is being sealed.

There is nothing to be gained by trying to reconcile this profoundly theological statement, at the historical level, with Mark's claim that Jesus was crucified at 9am (Mk 15:25). According to

Mark, 'darkness came over the whole land' at noon (Mk 15:33).

> *19:15 They cried out, 'Away with him! Away with him! Crucify him!' Pilate asked them, 'Shall I crucify your King?' The chief priests answered, 'We have no king but the emperor.'*

With considerable irony, on the eve of a feast celebrating the liberation of their people from oppression, the chief priests pass judgment on themselves. In declaring that they have no king but the emperor (the hated Tiberius Caesar), they commit the very crime of blasphemy that they attribute to Jesus. 'It is', as Duke (1985:135) remarks, 'a sacrilege no Jew could utter without forfeit of faith.' Indeed, it merited the death penalty as indicated in the verse we quoted earlier from Leviticus.

The irony is the more terrible when we recall that later in the evening, as Meeks (1967:77) reminds us, they will sing at the conclusion of the Greater Hallel:

> *From everlasting to everlasting thou art God;*
> ***Beside thee we have no king,*** *redeemer or saviour,*
> *No liberator, deliverer, provider;*
> *None who takes pity in every time of distress*
>   *and trouble.*
> ***We have no king but thee*** *(cf. Is 26:13; 1 Sam 8:7).*
> *(emphasis mine)*

There is further irony in the fact that, by the time the Fourth Gospel was written (probably a little after 90 C.E.), Jerusalem and its beautiful Temple had been destroyed by the Romans. The kingship of the emperor was then even more unquestioned.

What a terrible price Pilate has exacted from the chief priests in return for Jesus — nothing less than the public repudiation of their hope in a Messianic king.

19:16a Then he handed him over to them to be crucified ...

Without formally passing the death sentence on Jesus, Pilate hands him over (cf. 18:30) to the will of his enemies. This is not a defeat for Jesus; he had foreknowledge of his fate (cf. 13:1,3; 18:4).

As a parting comment on the trial before Pilate, let us listen to Culpepper's (1983:143) sage remarks about one whom we call to mind every time we recite the Creed:

Like other characters caught between the Jews and Jesus (principally Nicodemus, the lame man, and the blind man), Pilate is a study in the impossibility of compromise, the inevitability of decision, and the consequences of each alternative ... The reader who tries to temporize or escape through the gate of indecision will find Pilate as his companion along that path.

4. The way of the cross:
The crucifixion of Jesus (19:16b-37)

19:16b ... So they took Jesus; 17 and carrying the cross by himself, he went out to what is called The Place of the Skull, which in Hebrew is called Golgotha.

We are not told explicitly who lead Jesus away from the praetorium; but it is almost certainly a detail of Roman soldiers. There will be no need for them to press Simon of Cyrene into service (cf. Mt 27:32 // Mk 15:21 // Lk 23:26) because Jesus, always master of his own destiny in this Gospel, carries his own cross to Golgotha (cf. Gen 22:6 — Isaac). He lays down his life of his own accord (cf. 10:17-18).

For Jesus the cross, so despised by the Romans, is an instrument of victory as the beautiful Holy Week hymn reminds us ('Vexilla regis prodeunt, fulget crucis mysterium').

John alone mentions Golgotha by name (cf. 19:13 — Gabbatha). Our more familiar designation, Calvary, is derived from *'Calvaria'* (Latin for 'skull').

19:18 There they crucified him, and with him two others, one on either side, with Jesus between them.

The two men crucified with Jesus are identified by Matthew and Mark as 'bandits' (Mt 27:38 // Mk 15:27); Luke calls them 'criminals' (Lk 23:33). In all four Gospels the central position in this sorry tableau is assigned to Jesus.

For his part, John pays scant attention to those who share Jesus' fate and who are, in popular belief, accursed by God (cf. Deut 21:22-23; Gal 3:13). We are not told by him, for example, that they joined in the chorus of derision directed at Jesus (cf. Mt 27:39-44 // Mk 15:29-32 // Lk 23:35-39).

19:19 Pilate also had an inscription written and put on the cross. It read, 'Jesus of Nazareth, the King of the Jews.'

It was customary for criminals (or for others walking ahead of them) to carry to the place of execution an inscription naming the offender and giving details of the crime committed. Ironically, Jesus of Nazareth, who had fled when people wished to make him their king, is proclaimed 'the King of the Jews'.

19:20 Many of the Jews read this inscription, because the place where Jesus was crucified was near the city; and it was written in Hebrew, in Latin, and in Greek.

All four evangelists, in greater or lesser detail, mention this inscription (cf. Mt 27:37 // Mk 15:26 // Lk 23:38). However, John alone attributes it directly to Pilate and notes that it was written in Hebrew (the language of the people), Latin (the administrative language of the Romans) and Greek (the cultural, literary language).

The fact that many people were able to read the inscription on Jesus' cross may be symbolic of the universal saving significance of his death. He is indeed the king of all humankind who, now that he is lifted up, draws all people to himself (cf. 12:32).

19:21 Then the chief priests of the Jews said to Pilate, 'Do not write, "The King of the Jews," but, "This man said, I am King of the Jews." '

In this verse, unique to the Fourth Gospel, we see the chief priests, whom John constantly implicates in the death of Jesus, persevering in their unbelief to the end.

The repeated use of the phrase 'King of the Jews' works subliminally on the reader of the Gospel.

19:22 Pilate answered, 'What I have written I have written.'

Pilate is scornful both of the priests who ask that the inscription be changed and of those people who are foolish enough to take it seriously. Unwittingly, in proclaiming Jesus to be 'the King of the Jews', he has told the truth.

Christ's clothing

19:23 When the soldiers had crucified Jesus, they took his clothes and divided them into four parts, one for each soldier. They also took his tunic; now the tunic was seamless, woven in one piece from the top.

It was customary for the executioners to take possession of the clothing of the criminal, perhaps by casting lots for it (cf. Mt 27:35 // Mk 15:24 // Lk 23:34).

In Jesus' case we might see this as the fulfilment of prophecy:

They stare and gloat over me;
they divide my clothes among themselves,
and for my clothing they cast lots (Ps 22:17b-18).

However, John is more interested in the symbolism of these events than he is in prophetic fulfilment.

Alone among the evangelists, John states that the garments were divided four ways among the soldiers present. According to Ellis (1984:270),

'The number four . . . symbolises universality. What happens in Jesus' death happens for the sake of all — he is the Lamb of God, who takes away the sin of the world.'

The seamless tunic, to which John alone makes reference, is seen by some commentators as an allusion to the seamless robe which was worn by the high priest and which was ordinarily not to be torn (Lev 21:10; cf. Ex 28:31-35; Lev 16:4). However, as Jesus' priesthood is not an important theme in the Fourth Gospel, this interpretation is of dubious value.

Other scholars, taking account of the net in 21:11 which does not tear, even when filled with 153 large fish, believe that the seamless tunic may have ecclesiological significance and symbolise the essential unity of the Church. In this connection, de la Potterie (1989:129) draws our attention to the interpretation of St Augustine (*Tract. in Joann.,* 118:4):

> *The clothing of our Lord Jesus Christ divided into four parts represents his Church distributed in four parts, spread throughout the world . . . It gradually establishes itself everywhere . . . As for the tunic for which lots were cast, that symbolizes the unity of all the parts together in the bond of charity.*

This explanation has the advantage of touching on one of the themes of the Gospel (cf. 10:16;

11:51-52; 17:21-24). Jesus' prayer for his disciples is that 'they may become completely one' as he and the Father are one (17:22-23).

The rending of a garment in the Hebrew Scriptures is a way of symbolising division in the community (cf. 1 Kings 11:29-31). As nothing is more calculated to create schism in a believing community than the utterance of blasphemy, it is not surprising that the high priest, Caiaphas, reacts to Jesus' testimony in the trial scene described by two of the Synoptic writers by tearing his clothes (cf. Mt 26:65 // Mk 14:63).

19:24 So they said to one another, 'Let us not tear it, but cast lots for it to see who will get it.' This was to fulfil what the scripture says, 'They divided my clothes among themselves, and for my clothing they cast lots.'

19:25a And that is what the soldiers did ...

The quotation in 19:24 is from Psalm 22:18. It is alluded to by the other evangelists as well (cf. Mt 27:35 // Mk 15:24 // Lk 23:34).

Jesus' Mother and the beloved disciple

19:25b ... Meanwhile, standing near the cross of Jesus were his mother, and his mother's sister, Mary the wife of Clopas, and Mary Magdalene.

It is not immediately clear how many women are referred to in the verse which introduces the third of the five scenes which describe Jesus' crucifixion and death on Calvary. If it is the writer's intention to parallel the women and the soldiers who divide the clothing of Jesus among themselves, we would settle for four (as in the Syriac tradition).

According to John, who is the only evangelist to mention the presence of the mother of Jesus, the women stand not at a distance (cf. Mt 27: 55-56 // Mk 15:40-41; Lk 23:49) but 'near the cross'.

This is the first appearance of Mary, the mother of Jesus, in the Fourth Gospel since the marriage feast at Cana. As we shall see, there are literary parallels, rich in symbolic/theological content, between that story and the pericope under consideration.

19:26 When Jesus saw his mother and the disciple whom he loved standing beside her, he said to his mother, 'Woman, here is your son.'

Once more we see a Jesus who is still very much in control of the situation and who is solicitous for the welfare of his loved ones (cf. 18:8). However, at a deeper level, John is drawing our attention to something more than filial piety or solicitude.

Addressing his mother by the unusual (but not disrespectful) title of 'woman', as he did at Cana, Jesus points to a relationship which is even more fundamental than that established by ties of blood. In Forestell's (1974:87) words, 'A new Christian family is being assembled around the cross of Jesus.' Henceforth those who stand in closest relation to him will be, in the Synoptic terminology, those who hear the word of God and do the Father's will (cf. Mt 12:50 // Mk 3:35 // Lk 8:21).

19:27 Then he said to the disciple, 'Here is your mother.' And from that hour the disciple took her into his own home.

Both the mother of Jesus (John never mentions her by name) and the beloved disciple are given special offices. Jesus' 'hour' (cf. 2:4) has become their hour as well.

How fitting it is, as Navone and Cooper (1986: 297) point out, 'that she who gave birth to Jesus should be present at the birth of his new community.' Here in the midst of great sadness, Mary becomes (in the understanding of many spiritual writers) the mother of all Christians who are personified by the beloved disciple. Implicit in this notion of Mary's spiritual maternity is the belief that we, through faith, are truly brothers and sisters of Jesus.

Our interpretation of this verse calls to mind the following words from Jesus' supper discourse: 'When a woman is in labor, she has pain, because her hour has come. But when her child is born, she no longer remembers the anguish because of the joy of having brought a human being into the world' (16:21; cf. Is 66:7-11).

Not without good reason did the Second Vatican Council proclaim Mary to be 'Mother of the Church'.

The death of Jesus

19:28 After this, when Jesus knew that all was now finished, he said (in order to fulfill the scripture), 'I am thirsty.'

At the risk of being repetitious, let us note once more that the spotlight remains on Jesus. John studiously avoids such 'distractions' as the blasphemies of the by-standers, the rebuke of the thieves, and the derision of the chief priests.

His Jesus does not cry out to the Father as one forsaken (cf. Mt 27:46 // Mk 15:34); nor does he expire with a loud cry (cf. Mt 27:50 // Mk 15:37 // Lk 23:46). Rather, in words peculiar to the Fourth Gospel, Jesus gives voice to a thirst which is at once physical and 'Messianic' (cf. 4:7-10).

Our source of the water which assuages the deepest of all human thirsts, he himself 'thirsts for God, for the living God' (Ps 42:2; cf. 63:1) and for the completion of the mission the Father has entrusted to him.

19:29 A jar full of sour wine was standing there. So they put a sponge full of the wine on a branch of hyssop and held it to his mouth.

Whereas Jesus provided superior quality wine at Cana (2:10), he is offered in his agony some of the poor wine (cf. Ps 69:21) which the soldiers may have brought to quench their own thirst. The full import of Jesus' 'I am thirsty' has, not surprisingly, escaped them. The wine is offered to him in a sponge supported on 'a branch of hyssop' (Matthew and Mark refer to 'a stick' — Mt 27:48 // Mk 15:36).

The fact that a stalk of hyssop would hardly support a sponge might lead us to look for a symbolic interpretation of this detail. John may be alluding to the fact that hyssop was used in sprinkling the blood of the Passover lamb (Ex 12:22; cf. Heb 9:19). This is in keeping with the Johannine emphasis on the Passover theme (cf. 19:36).

19:30 When Jesus had received the wine, he said, 'It is finished.' Then he bowed his head and gave up his spirit.

Not content to remark that Jesus 'breathed his last' (Mt 27:50//Mk 15:37//Lk 23:46),[7] John states that he 'gave up his spirit.' This expression (rendered 'handed over his spirit' in the revised (1986) NAB translation) may carry a double burden of meaning. It could refer both to the physical death of Jesus and to his gift of the Holy Spirit, 'another Advocate' (14:16), in fulfilment of his promise (cf. 7:37-39; 16:7).

In one of the post-resurrection appearances we are told more explicitly of the disciples' reception of the Spirit (20:22).

As he dies Jesus gives voice to what might be called a cry of victory, 'It is finished.' For Navone and Cooper (1986:276) these words 'are the signature to his entire life's work'. His is not a passive death but the serene acceptance of the consequences of his fidelity to the will of his Father (cf. 14:31). In Jesus' final utterance we have an echo of his earlier statements:

*'My food is to do the will of him who sent me and to **complete his work**' (4:34).*
*'I glorified you on earth by **finishing the work** that you gave me to do' (17:4). (emphasis mine)*

---

7 Luke adds Jesus' words, 'Father, into your hands I commend my spirit.'

With good reason, there is no mention in the Johannine passion narrative of the sinister darkness which descends upon the land as Jesus dies (cf. Mt 27:45 // Mk 15:33 // Lk 23:44). This would hardly be in keeping with this evangelist's understanding of Jesus' death as the moment of his glorification. 'The light shines in the darkness, and the darkness did not overcome it' (1:5).

The blood and water

19:31 *Since it was the day of Preparation, the Jews did not want the bodies left on the cross during the sabbath, especially because that sabbath was a day of great solemnity. So they asked Pilate to have the legs of the crucified men broken and the bodies removed.*

The scene which this verse introduces is found only in John. There is no mention in the Synoptic writings of the flow of blood and water from Jesus' side or of the breaking of the legs of the two men crucified with him.

To keep the land free of the uncleanness that attached to the body of a crucified person, the law required that the remains be disposed of on the day of death. In Deut 21:22-23 we read:

When someone is convicted of a crime punishable by death and is executed, and you hang him on a tree, his corpse must not remain all night upon the tree; you shall bury him that same day, for anyone hung on a tree is under God's curse. You must not defile the land that the LORD your God is giving you for possession (cf. Jos 8:29; 10:26-27).

There was an added sense of urgency in the case of Jesus' burial as the Friday on which he died was the day before the Passover (a sabbath day in that year). This explains the Jews' request that the death be hastened by the breaking of his legs (the *crurifragium* as this customary act of 'mercy' is called).

It is interesting to note that, though the Jewish authorities question Pilate in the praetorium, the evangelist manages to keep the focus of our attention on Calvary.

19:32 Then the soldiers came and broke the legs of the first and of the other who had been crucified with him.

The breaking of the legs expedited the dying process by inducing suffocation. Without this intervention a condemned man might live for several days on the cross.

19:33 But when they came to Jesus and saw that he was already dead, they did not break his legs.

The fact that Jesus is already dead may point to the severity of the scourging he endured

(19:1). In any event, it is important to John for theological reasons that the legs of Jesus should not be broken (cf. 19:36; Ex 12:46; Num 9:12).

> *19:34 Instead, one of the soldiers pierced his side with a spear, and at once blood and water came out.*

One of the Roman soldiers, perhaps in an effort to make doubly sure that the Nazarene is dead, thrusts his spear deep into the side of Jesus (cf. 20:27), thereby initiating a flow of blood and water (cf. 1 Jn 5:6-9). John's reference to this occurrence may, as some writers have pointed out, reflect ancient medical views concerning bodily fluids. However, the evangelist's concern is certainly theological.

In the first place the flow of blood and water affirms, against the heresy of the Docetists (who claimed that Jesus had only the appearance of a human body), the reality of Jesus' death (cf. 1 Jn 1:1). Moreover, in view of the fact that Jesus dies at the very time that the lambs are being slaughtered in the Temple for the Passover observance, it is plausible to see the blood which flows from his side as the sacrificial blood of the saving 'Lamb of God' (1:29,36; cf. 1 Jn 1:7; 2:2; Heb 9:12).

Doubtless, John's readers would have seen some Eucharistic symbolism in the blood shed for them on Calvary (cf. 6:53-56).[8]

The flow of water recalls many elements of Jesus' teaching (3:5; 4:14; 7:37-39; cf. Rev 22:1); and, in the light of this teaching, we may see it as symbolic both of baptism and of the Holy Spirit who dwells in the baptised person as in a temple.

Ellis (1984:276) suggests that there may also be an allusion to the life-giving water that flowed from Ezekiel's new temple (Ezek 47:1-12; cf. Jn 2:13-25).

19:35 (He who saw this has testified so that you also may believe. His testimony is true, and he knows that he tells the truth.)

This verse, which is similar to 21:24 (cf. 1 Jn 5:6-8), is probably a later editorial addition to the text. Though the eye-witness referred to is presumably the beloved disciple of 19:26, we

8 Jewish law forbade the consumption of blood. In Leviticus 17:11 we read: 'For the life of the flesh is in the blood; and I have given it to you for making atonement for your lives on the altar; for, as life, it is the blood that makes atonement' (cf. Deut 12:23). However, in the Christian understanding of the Eucharist, we consume the blood of Christ (poured out in atonement for our sins) that we might have his life in us.

cannot conclude from this fact that he is the writer of the Gospel.

The clause, 'so that you also may believe', has pastoral overtones (cf. 20:31; 1 Jn 5:13). John is reminding the fence-sitters in his community and the 'crypto-Christians' that, in the flow of blood and water, they should recognise one of the most precious of Jesus' signs — a symbolic witness both to the truth of the Lord's teaching and to the efficacy of the sacraments of baptism and the Eucharist.

19:36 These things occurred so that the scripture might be fulfilled, 'None of his bones shall be broken.'

The scripture text in question is to be found in the book of Exodus: '[The passover lamb] shall be eaten in one house; you shall not take any of the animal outside the house, and you shall not break any of its bones' (Ex 12:46; cf. Num 9:12; Ps 34:20).

In his discourse on the day after the miracle of the loaves and fish, Jesus spoke about the need to consume his flesh (6:52-58). He himself is the new Passover lamb (cf. 1 Cor 5:7).

19:37 And again another passage of scripture says, 'They will look on the one whom they have pierced.'

John is here quoting from a passage in the writings of the prophet Zechariah:

And I will pour out a spirit of compassion and supplication on the house of David and the inhabitants of Jerusalem, so that, when they look on the one whom they have pierced, they shall mourn for him, as one mourns for an only child, and weep bitterly over him, as one weeps over a firstborn (Zech 12:10; cf. Rev 1:7; Ps 22:17).

5. The burial of Jesus (19:38-42)

19:38 After these things, Joseph of Arimathea, who was a disciple of Jesus, though a secret one because of his fear of the Jews, asked Pilate to let him take away the body of Jesus. Pilate gave him permission; so he came and removed his body.

Joseph of Arimathea (a small Judean town about 100km from Jerusalem) is mentioned by all four evangelists as the one who approached Pilate to ask for Jesus' body. He is variously described as 'a disciple of Jesus' (Mt 27:57), as 'a respected member of the council, who was also himself waiting expectantly for the kingdom of God' (Mk 15:43), and as 'a good and righteous man ... who, though a member of the council, had not agreed to their plan and action' (Lk 23:50-51).

John alone adds, rather characteristically, that Joseph was one of Jesus' secret disciples 'because of his fear of the Jews'. This being so, it seems that, like the disciples on Pentecost day, he has already found new courage and strength in the Spirit.

His intervention (cf. Acts 8:2) saves the body of Jesus from the final indignity of being consigned to a common burial ground.

19:39 Nicodemus, who had at first come to Jesus by night, also came, bringing a mixture of myrrh and aloes, weighing about a hundred pounds.

Though it is not explicitly stated, it is a reasonable assumption that Nicodemus too has become a secret disciple of Jesus. He had been more favourably disposed towards the rabbi he had first approached under cover of darkness (3:1-21) than the other members of the Sanhedrin (cf. 7:50-52).

There is no reference in the Synoptic Gospels to any embalming on the Friday of Jesus' death. In Mark (16:1) and Luke (24:1) the women come to the tomb with spices on Sunday morning precisely with this task in mind.

John, however, despite what must have been the hurried nature of the operation, has the body of Jesus immediately anointed for burial (cf. 12:7) in the extravagant fashion one would associate with the entombment of a king (cf. Ex 30:22-33; 2 Chron 16:14).

Myrrh and aloes were commonly used for this purpose; but 'a hundred pounds' must surely be accounted an enormous quantity to use in the burial of a crucified person. An average working man could not pay for it in a lifetime. Keep in mind that the workers in the vineyard (Mt 20:1-16) all receive the 'usual daily wage' of one denarius and that the 'pound of costly perfume made of pure nard' (12:3), which Mary uses to anoint Jesus' feet, is valued by Judas at 'three hundred denarii' (12:5; cf. 6:7).

19:40 They took the body of Jesus and wrapped it with the spices in linen cloths, according to the burial custom of the Jews.

While all the Synoptic Gospels refer to Jesus' linen burial garment (cf. Mt 27:59 // Mk 15:46 // Lk 23:53), there is a special element in the Johannine account. Looking forward to the glorious resurrection of Jesus, the evangelist would doubtless have us recall, as we read the above verse, the miracle of the raising of Lazarus (cf. 11:44).

19:41 Now there was a garden in the place where he was crucified, and in the garden there was a new tomb in which no one had ever been laid.

83

Jesus is buried in a new rock-hewn tomb 'in which no one had ever been laid' (cf. Lk 23:53). According to Matthew, it belongs to Joseph of Arimathea (Mt 27:60).

The fact that Jesus' burial takes place in a garden is a detail peculiar to the Fourth Gospel. As Jesus was arrested in a garden, this serves as a kind of inclusion-conclusion to the whole passion narrative.

19:42 And so, because it was the Jewish day of Preparation, and the tomb was nearby, they laid Jesus there.

The tenor of this text suggests that the burial arrangements are only temporary. This would explain the mission of the women on Easter Sunday morning in the Synoptic Gospels.

Part 2

A Johannine Way of the Cross

An introductory reflection

I prefer to use the term 'way of the cross' to designate the total spiritual exercise we are about to consider and the word 'stations' to denote the various stopping places along the way. The reason for this is that the word 'way' has overtones which are quite significant for our lives as disciples of Christ.

We commonly speak of life as a journey; and, in the terminology of Vatican II's Dogmatic Constitution on the Church *(Lumen Gentium)*, we sometimes refer to ourselves as a 'pilgrim people' who have responded positively to Jesus' call to follow him. Like the Chosen People, who were exhorted to 'walk humbly with [their] God' (Mic 6:8), we are called to travel 'the good and the right way' (1 Sam 12:23; cf. Ps 101:2,6; Prov 2:20) which leads to life rather than 'the way of the wicked' (Ps 1:6; cf. Prov 12:28; 21:8) which leads to death.

Matthew reminds his community that 'the gate is narrow and the road is hard that leads to life' (Mt 7:14; cf. Lk 13:24). In this connection, it is interesting to note how often in the Synoptic Gospels people actually meet Jesus on the road and are challenged to have faith in him (among other examples, consider Lk 9:57-62; 24:13-33; cf. Acts 8:26-40; 9:3-9 and 22:6-11).

John goes a step further than the Synoptic writers. For him Jesus is not simply the guide, escort and leader of all who would walk in the ways of the Lord (cf. Ps 119:1-5; 128:1); he is the way just as (and, indeed, because) he is the truth and the life (14:6a). He alone provides access to the Father in whose house he will prepare a dwelling place for his own (14:2-3). 'No one comes to the Father except through me' (14:6b), Jesus states quite unequivocally in his farewell discourse at the Last Supper.

As is so often the case in the Fourth Gospel, the disciples are uncomprehending (cf. 14:5). In particular, they do not appreciate the fact that the path to the heavenly Jerusalem leads along the way of the cross which Jesus must soon tread in the streets of the earthly Jerusalem.

Later, after the risen Lord has said to him, 'Follow me' (21:19,22), Peter will realise that, on the way to glory, there are no detours open to the true believer. Writing in his first epistle about the cost of discipleship, he says: 'For to this have you been called, because Christ also suffered for you, leaving you an example, so that you should follow in his steps' (1 Pet 2:21; cf. Mt 16:24//Mk 8:34//Lk 9:23; Lk 24:26).

For some of those who did follow in Jesus' footsteps, 'the Way' became almost a synonym for the faith they professed. Paul, for example, when he is on trial before the governor, Felix, states boldly: 'But this I admit to you, that according to **the Way**, which they [the Jews] call a sect, I worship the God of our ancestors, . . . ' (Acts 24:14 *[emphasis mine]*; cf. Acts 9:2; 18:26; 19:9,23; 22:4; 24:22).

As we move from station to station in the Johannine Way of the Cross presented below, reflecting on the Christ who still suffers in our midst today, we should see more clearly the aptness of the term, 'the Way', to describe the Christian life. We may also find ourselves echoing the sentiments of Pierre Teilhard de Chardin (1977: 342): 'The human epic resembles nothing so much as a way of the Cross.'

Historical background

Though much of the city of Jerusalem was destroyed by the Romans in 70 C.E., generations of Jesus' followers continued to identify and to venerate the places connected with his life, especially those which evoked memories of his passion, death and resurrection. Not surprisingly, pilgrimages to these places were undertaken, in a spirit of devotion and penitence, very early in the history of the Christian Church. For those who travelled from afar, such journeys were costly and often fraught with danger; and, for these reasons, a pilgrimage to the Holy Land was commonly considered to be a once-in-a-lifetime experience for a privileged few.

During the crusades many churches were built on sites associated with the sacred mysteries of our Lord's life; and, as the crusaders and pilgrims returned to their own countries, similar commemorative shrines were erected throughout Europe. This served as a stimulus to the faith of the people, most of whom could not hope to visit the land of Jesus; and it also gave added impetus to the growing devotion to the passion of Christ.

By the 15th century, a series of such shrines or tableaux recalling the events of Jesus' passion was to be found in many Christian churches and oratories and sometimes also in cemeteries. The devotion that we call the Way of the Cross grew up; and it was popularised by the ubiquitous Franciscans who had assumed custody of the holy places in 1342.

The Way of the Cross has had a varied history in Jerusalem itself where there has never been general agreement among different groups of Christians as to the actual route followed by Jesus to Calvary. As Murphy-O'Connor (1986:

33) succinctly expresses it: 'The Via Dolorosa is defined by faith, not by history.'

Nor has there been unanimity of practice elsewhere with respect to the number and titles of the stations. They have varied in number from five to more than thirty and have included events in our Lord's life that have little relevance to his passion. Some of the stations chosen, for example the repeated falls of Jesus (seven in one listing) and the ministrations of Veronica, are without biblical warrant. However, a series of 14 stations was eventually adopted rather generally, possibly because of the influence of a few widely respected devotional manuals.

Modern approaches

With the approval (and, I believe, the encouragement) of the Holy See, there is a movement today, at least in some parts of the world, to adopt a more strictly biblical Way of the Cross and to include the resurrection of Jesus as the final station. A good example has been set in this matter by the recently refurbished Cathedral of St Stephen in my home town of Brisbane, Australia.

Some people would query the appropriateness of commemorating the resurrection in the Way of the Cross, especially on Good Friday. While I am sure that good arguments could be adduced for and against this practice, it remains true that we cannot separate theologically the death of Jesus from his resurrection. It is with faith in Jesus risen that we come to make the Way of the Cross in the first place.

A Johannine model

With these thoughts in mind, I have outlined in the pages which follow a new set of ten stations, for personal or community use, based on St John's Gospel. They are as follows:

1. Jesus raises Lazarus from the dead (11:1-44).
2. Jesus washes his disciples' feet (13:1-17).
3. The arrest of Jesus in the garden (18:1-11).
4. Jesus before Annas (18:12-27).
5. The trial of Jesus before Pilate (18:28—19:16a).
6. The crucifixion of Jesus (19:16b-25a).
7. Jesus' commission to Mary and the beloved disciple (19:25b-27).
8. Jesus gives up his spirit (19:28-37).
9. Jesus' body is entombed (19:38-42).
10. The risen Jesus appears to Mary Magdalen (20:1-18).

I have chosen to commence the journey of Jesus to Calvary at the tomb of Lazarus near the village of Bethany, two miles outside Jerusalem. My justification for this choice is that, in the Fourth Gospel, the raising of Lazarus is the beginning of the end for Jesus. The evangelist states quite bluntly that 'from that day on they planned to put him to death' (11:53).

Because the Lazarus event points towards the resurrection of Jesus and is theologically linked to it, there is a certain appropriateness in ending our Way of the Cross with the first of the post-resurrection appearances recorded by John. On both of these occasions Jesus, the life-giver, brings peace, consolation and abundant joy to a weeping Mary at a tomb.

Just as the concluding station directs our thoughts to the triumph of Easter Day, so also the second station invites us to reflect on the self-emptying of Jesus in the washing of the feet of his disciples on Holy Thursday. In this way our Good Friday service reflects the essential unity of the Sacred Triduum.

We may note in passing that the washing of the feet in the Fourth Gospel exercises a similar function to the institution of the Eucharist in Matthew and Luke. In both of these symbolic actions Jesus interprets the saving character of his sacrificial death before it happens.

If used in a parish setting on Good Friday, the ten Johannine stations would have the advantage of aligning the time-honoured devotional exercise of the Way of the Cross with the prescribed Gospel reading of that day.

I leave it to the ingenuity of the parish liturgy committee to work out how this can be done when their church has already invested in (and made constant use of) a set of the traditional artistic representations of Jesus' passion. A class I once had the privilege of teaching wrote their own texts for reflective prayer on Jesus' passion and, using a variety of techniques (including collage), produced a rather modern series of images for a Way of the Cross.

Only the essential material for a Good Friday prayer service has been included in the pages which follow. It suggests as a basic structure:

(a) The announcement of the station by a leader.
(b) The reading of the material provided. (A number of good readers could be used.)
(c) A pause to allow personal reflection in silence.
(d) A prayer said in common by all present.

Other traditional elements (such as an introductory prayer, suitable hymns/music, a 'linking' sentence as one moves from one station to the next, and a concluding prayer) have been left to leave to the discretion of those who presumably know local customs and conditions best — the liturgy committee or some such body. The following suggestions may be of some assistance to the planners.

As introductory prayers, Psalms 51 *(Miserere)* and 130 *(De profundis)* might be considered. In making these prayers our own we humbly and gratefully acknowledge that we, who have been exposed to the mystery of evil, have also been exposed to the consoling mystery of God's compassion. What better dispositions could we have as we begin our Way of the Cross than sincere repentance for our sins and unshakeable hope that the God of steadfast love will forgive us.

As 'linking' prayers, three which commend themselves to me are:

Lord, by your cross and resurrection you have set us free; you are the Saviour of the world.

We adore you, O Christ, and we praise you because by your holy cross and resurrection you have redeemed the world.

Lord Jesus, for our sake you 'became obedient to the point of death — even death on a cross' (Phil 2:8).

At the conclusion of the exercise one might pray simply the Apostles' Creed or the *Anima*

Christi, a prayer which closely links Jesus' passion with the Eucharistic sacrifice. Much loved by St Ignatius Loyola, this latter prayer is probably best known as the hymn, 'Soul of my Saviour ... '.

Ordinarily, in making the Way of the Cross, I would prefer to take the readings directly from the Sacred Scripture. However, as John 18-19 is read in full in the Celebration of the Lord's Passion which begins at 3 pm on Good Friday, I feel that it would be better not to include the actual text of these chapters in a Johannine Way of the Cross held earlier in the day.

First station
Jesus raises Lazarus from the dead (11:1-44)

In a deliberately belated response to the plea of
two of his dear friends, the sisters Martha and
Mary, Jesus has come to Bethany in company
with homas and some of his other disciples.
e stands amid a crowd of mourners before the
cave tomb of Lazarus — a loved one four days
dead.

He who came that we might have abundant
life (10:10) confronts the awful reality of death.
He who would have his joy in us so that our joy
might be complete (15:11) stands in the midst of
human grief.

Touched to the very depths of his being, Jesus
weeps: tears of love for his departed friend, tears
of compassion for those who mourn his death,
tears of horror at the prospect of what he himself must endure in Jerusalem — the place where
prophets die (cf. Mt 23:37-38; 1 Thess 2:15).

He prays to his Father; the bystanders roll back
the stone at his command; Lazarus comes forth
in obedience to his call; and the glory of God
is revealed (cf. 11:4). Many who witness this
miraculous sign come to believe in Jesus (11:45).

For the leaders of the people this is the last straw; from this day on they plan to put him to death (11:53).

Jesus, brother and friend, as the Father loves you so also do you love us. Free us, we pray, from all that is life-diminishing. Call us forth from the dark prison of our selfishness and complacent sinfulness into the light of your grace and truth. Unbind us that we may live henceforth in your love, filled with your life-giving Spirit.

Second station
Jesus washes his disciples' feet (13:1-17)

In Jerusalem for the Passover feast, Jesus sits at table with his disciples for the last time. He knows that soon he must depart from this world and return to his Father. The long-awaited hour he has often spoken about has come. On the next day he will be lifted up on the cross, shamed in the eyes of the world but glorified in the presence of his heavenly Father.

Towards the end of the meal, Jesus removes his outer garment, a seamless robe such as the high priest was required to wear. He ties a towel around his waist and, despite the protestations of Peter, he proceeds to wash his disciples' feet.

In this act of exemplary humility Jesus subverts the world of established power relationships, reveals the extravagant love of God, provides those present with a model of servant leadership, prepares them to accept the notion of a crucified Messiah and interprets his saving death before it actually happens.

Tonight he pours water into a bowl; tomorrow he will pour out his very life for them.

Jesus, master and servant, wash us yet again who have been baptised in your name. Cleanse us of all that would prevent us from having a disciple's share with you. Empower us with the living water of your Spirit so that, following your example and observing your ordinance, we may wash one another's feet in loving and generous service.

Third station
The arrest of Jesus in the garden (18:1-11)

After the supper, Jesus and his disciples cross the Kidron valley and enter a garden where they have often met together. Jesus knows that this place of intimacy is about to become a place of infamy.

Armed to the teeth, a detail of Roman soldiers and temple guards, accompanied by the traitor Judas, are approaching to arrest him, the one whose gift to us is heavenly peace (14:27). When they emerge from the darkness, holding lanterns and torches aloft, Jesus of Nazareth, the light of the world (8:12; 9:5), steps forward; and these lackeys of imperial power fall at his feet.

Jesus rejects Peter's attempt to defend him by violent means. As his hour has now come, he will go to death and glory willingly. 'No one takes [my life] from me,' he had once said, 'but I lay it down of my own accord. I have power to lay it down, and I have power to take it up again' (10:18).

The soldiers bind Jesus, who nonetheless remains the only truly free person present, and lead him away like a common criminal to the high priest's house.

Jesus, ever faithful to the mission entrusted to you by your heavenly Father, you handed yourself over to the forces of sin and death so that we might have abundant life. May we never betray you by embracing worldly values or by failing to recognise you in our brothers and sisters who, in your name, suffer persecution for the sake of justice.

Fourth station
Jesus before Annas (18:12-27)

Jesus of Nazareth, the religious tradition's most authentic representative, stands before Annas, the wily powerbroker of the religious establishment. He is on trial for his life; but sentence has already been passed on him. His inquisitor's son-in-law, the high priest Caiaphas, has said, 'It is better for you to have one man die for the people than to have the whole nation destroyed' (11:50).

Jesus stands his ground with exemplary courage; and, with the self-assurance that arises from true authority, he responds to Annas's questions about his teaching ministry. His forthrightness is too much for one of the police present who, unable to distinguish between composure and insolence, strikes Jesus in the face.

Elsewhere, in the courtyard of the high priest, a trial of another kind is taking place. Confronted with the repeated challenge to witness to his master, Peter fails the test of discipleship. His weakness is in marked contrast with the strength that Jesus consistently displays throughout his passion.

A crowing cock announces the fulfilment of Jesus' prophecy that Peter would deny him.

Jesus, our model and guide, enrich us ever more with the gifts of your Holy Spirit. As we face the trials of daily life, give us the fortitude to confess our faith in you openly as disciples worthy of the name. Strengthen those of our contemporaries whose faithful Christian witness inspires hatred in their persecutors and hope in us.

Fifth station
The trial of Jesus before Pilate (18:28—19:16a)

Having been sent bound from Annas to Caiaphas, Jesus is finally taken early in the morning
of the Jewish day of Preparation for the Passover
to stand trial at the headquarters of the Roman
governor, Pontius Pilate. An expectant crowd, including some of the chief priests, gathers outside intent on Jesus' execution by crucifixion.

In his dealings with this group of people and
in his questioning of Jesus, Pilate persistently refers
to the accused as the King of the Jews. Unaware of
the irony of his chosen title, Pilate thus attempts
to taunt the mob and to humiliate Jesus himself.

At one point, after he has had him cruelly
scourged, he presents Jesus to them mockingly
crowned with thorns and wearing a robe of royal
purple. 'Here is the man!' he says to them. 'Here
is your King!'

The chief priests blasphemously proclaim that
they have no king but the emperor and call for
Jesus to be put to death. Though he has experienced something like awe in the presence of
Jesus, whose innocence he has thrice affirmed,
Pilate weakly yields to their pressure and hands
him over to them to be crucified.

Jesus, King and Christ, you came to bear witness to the truth by revealing to us who God is and who, with the help of your grace, we are called to become. May you always reign in our hearts so that, amid the trials of life, we may confess you without compromise and hold fast to your truth which alone has the power to save us.

Sixth station
The crucifixion of Jesus (19:16b-25a)

As Isaac obediently carried the wood of sacrifice to the mountain-top in the land of Moriah at the request of his father Abraham, so Jesus carries his cross to Calvary, the Place of the Skull. There, along with two others, he is subjected to the barbarity of crucifixion by four despised Roman soldiers.

In fulfilment of prophecy and in keeping with custom, his executioners divide his clothing among themselves and cast lots for his robe. This garment, woven without seam, may be seen as symbolising, in its intactness, the essential unity of the Church for which Jesus prayed in his farewell discourse (17:20-23).

Much to the chagrin of his enemies, an inscription on the cross in Latin, Greek and Hebrew, affixed on the orders of Pilate, identifies him as 'Jesus of Nazareth, the King of the Jews'.

Jesus' prediction has at last been fulfilled that, hated without a cause (15:25), he would be lifted up on the cross of shame (3:14; 8:28; 12:32-33) and thereby be uplifted into the glory he had in the Father's presence before the world existed (17:5).

Jesus, loving saviour and merciful judge, you promised that when you should be lifted up on the cross you would draw all people to yourself. Gather together in the embrace of your saving love all those who do not yet know you so that, believing in your name, they may be gifted with eternal life.

Seventh station
Jesus' commission to Mary and the beloved disciple (19:25b-27)

Confronted with a sea of faces, some hostile, some disinterested, some merely curious, Jesus is aware of the presence of four women who have remained faithful to him to the end: Mary the wife of Clopas, Mary Magdalene, his grieving mother, and his mother's sister. Also standing at the foot of his cross is the beloved disciple, a man after Jesus' own heart.

As his life ebbs painfully away, Jesus, in a poignantly intimate scene, is moved to perform one of the last and most important acts of his earthly ministry. He says to his mother, addressing her as he did at Cana, 'Woman, here is your son.' Then to the beloved disciple he says, 'Here is your mother.'

With the assignment of these special roles to Mary of Nazareth and to our 'representative', a new family comes into being, 'born, not of blood or of the will of the flesh or of the will of man, but of God' (1:13).

Mary, who is Jesus' mother in the order of nature, thus becomes the mother not only of the beloved disciple but also of all God's children in the order of grace.

Jesus, through our baptism we have become children of God in a new and holy fellowship of faith, hope and love. Through the intercession of Mary, mother of the Church, we pray that we may be one even as you and the Father are one so that we may be a sign of your saving presence to those who do not yet know you.

Eighth station
Jesus gives up his spirit (19:28-37)

As the end approaches, Jesus says, 'I am thirsty' — words which the bystanders hear only as the anguished plea of a dying man. Unaware that his real thirst even now is to do his Father's will with the utmost fidelity, they hold to his lips a sponge soaked in wine of very poor quality.

'We must work the works of him who sent me while it is day', Jesus had said to his disciples; 'night is coming when no one can work' (9:4). He knows that this time is at last upon him and that his earthly mission is accomplished. No sooner has Jesus taken the wine offered to him than he says, 'It is finished.' Across the ages we hear these words with the ear of faith as a cry of triumph over the forces of evil. Dying, he has indeed destroyed our death.

Jesus bows his head; and, in obedience to his Father and in gift to Mary, the beloved disciple, the other faithful ones at the foot of the cross and to us, he hands over his spirit.

As a final indignity, Jesus' lifeless body is further mutilated, not by the breaking of his legs (as is the lot of those crucified with him) but by the thrust of a soldier's lance which causes blood and water to flow from his side.

110

Jesus, true God and true man, 'having loved [your] own who were in the world, [you] loved them to the end.' Filled with the wisdom of your Spirit, we know that in that love alone is our salvation. Give us the grace to respond with generous hearts so that your sacrifice on Calvary may bear abundant fruit in us.

Ninth station
Jesus' body is entombed (19:38-42)

It is necessary that Jesus' mortal remains should be disposed of without delay because it is now the afternoon of the Jewish day of Preparation for the Passover and the eve of the Great Sabbath. Mindful of the demands of the law and the requirements of ritual piety, Joseph of Arimathea, a member of the Sanhedrin who is secretly a disciple of Jesus, obtains Pilate's permission to remove the body of our Saviour from Calvary.

With the assistance of his friend and colleague Nicodemus, who has also come to believe in Jesus, he takes the body to a nearby garden in which there is a new tomb hewn in the rock. As we know from another source, it belongs to Joseph himself (Mt 27:60).

Then the one whom Pilate had consistently and contemptuously referred to as the King of the Jews is given a regal burial. Nicodemus's parting gift of about 100 pounds weight of very expensive spices, a mixture of myrrh and aloes, is used to embalm the body of Jesus as befits a king.

Having covered Jesus' face with a cloth and wrapped his body in linen cloths, Joseph and

Nicodemus seal the tomb and leave what they believe to be Jesus' last resting place.

[There is a certain appropriateness in the fact that, on the completion of his work of bringing a new creation into being, Jesus should rest in the sepulchre on the day of the Great Sabbath. Let us reflect in silence on this mystery of the divine life poured out for us in love.]

Tenth station
The risen Jesus appears to Mary Magdalen (20:1-18)

The darkness which envelops Mary Magdalen as she approaches the burial place of Jesus on the Sunday morning after his death is in keeping with her mood. Having entered the garden with a heavy heart, she is surprised to find the stone removed from the entrance to the tomb. In haste she runs to tell Peter and the beloved disciple of her disturbing discovery.

After they have confirmed the truth of her statement, Mary stands alone weeping outside the tomb. She bends down to look inside where she sees two angels dressed in white who ask her the cause of her tears. Having enquired of them if they know the whereabouts of her Lord, she turns away and, without recognising him, sees Jesus standing there.

In response to her repeated entreaty, Jesus simply says, 'Mary!' Beside herself with joy, she exclaims, 'Rabbouni!' which means Teacher. Jesus restrains her when she seeks to embrace him and sends her to announce to his disciples, 'I am ascending to my Father and your Father, to my God and your God.'

'I have seen the Lord', she says to them. It is the very first proclamation of the good news.

Lord Jesus, you are the first born of many brothers and sisters, our resurrection and our life. Because your tomb is empty our lives are full of hope that we will pass from death to life with you. Call us by name, as you called Mary of Magdala, so that we may rise to the challenge of discipleship in the strength of your love.

Part 3

The sorrowful mysteries of the Rosary: a Johannine version

Just as we traced briefly the evolution of the devotion we call the Way of the Cross, so also it would be possible to outline the development of another traditional exercise of piety, the Rosary. However, for our present purpose only a few historical observations would seem to be necessary.

As a pious practice among Christians, the Rosary spread throughout Europe, especially from the beginning of the 13th century. It is commonly believed, though the evidence is scant, that St Dominic (+ 1221) preached the devotion in response to a revelation he received from the Blessed Virgin. More certain is the fact that the Dominicans were foremost among those who popularised the Rosary as a simple method of prayer combining repetitive vocal elements with contemplation of the mysteries of Christ's life.

The number, name and configuration of the decades varied considerably from place to place until Pope Pius V (1566-72), himself a Dominican, issued a bull in 1569 which helped to standardise the Rosary in the form that we are accustomed to today. Four years later a feast of the Rosary was instituted which is celebrated annually on 7 October.

Over the centuries many popes have urged the faithful to recite the Rosary which is, in Pope

Pius XII's words, 'the compendium of the entire Gospel' (Letter to the Archbishop of Manila, *Philippinas Insulas:* AAS 38 (1946), p. 419). See, for example, Pope Paul VI's apostolic exhortation, *Marialis Cultus*, 1974, #42-55.

In the concluding paragraph of *Marialis Cultus* the Holy Father writes:

> *We desire . . . to recommend that this very worthy devotion should not be propagated in a way that is too one-sided or exclusive. The Rosary is an excellent prayer, but the faithful should feel supremely free in its regard. They should be drawn to its calm recitation by its intrinsic appeal.*

My practice of choosing alternative joyful, sorrowful and glorious mysteries of our Lord's life in my personal recitation of the Rosary is, I believe, fully consistent with the spirit of this statement.

The reader might like to use in his or her personal prayer or with a group the following Johannine version of the sorrowful mysteries:

• First mystery:
Jesus accepts the cup of suffering (18:1-11).

• Second mystery:
Jesus endures rejection and denial (18:12-27).

- Third mystery:
Jesus, our King, confronts Pilate (18:28—19:16a).

- Fourth mystery:
Jesus dies and is glorified (19:16b-37).

- Fifth mystery:
Jesus' body is regally entombed (19:38-42).

The usual prayers may be said in connection with each of these mysteries which presuppose familiarity with the Johannine passion narrative and some appreciation of the approach to Christology which informs the whole of the Fourth Gospel. Our commentary on chapters 18 and 19 of John should be helpful in this regard.

It may also be of assistance, as each decade of the Rosary is announced, to read aloud a pertinent verse or two of the Gospel and then to pause briefly with a view to focusing attention on the particular mystery. The following texts may serve as a guide:

- First mystery:
'Am I not to drink the cup that the Father has given me?' (18:11). Consider also: 18:4; 10:11; 10:17-18a; 15:13.

- Second mystery:
Jesus answered, 'If I have spoken wrongly, testify to the wrong. But if I have spoken rightly,

why do you strike me?' (18:23). Consider also:
18:17; 1:11.

● Third mystery:
Pilate asked him, 'So you are a king?' Jesus answered, 'You say that I am a king. For this I was born, and for this I came into the world, to testify to the truth' (18:37). Consider also: 19:2-3; 19:5; 19:14.

● Fourth mystery:
So they took Jesus; and carrying the cross by himself, he went out to what is called The Place of the Skull, ... There they crucified him ... (19:16b-18). Consider also: 19:26-27; 19:30; 19:34.

● Fifth mystery:
Now there was a garden in the place where he was crucified, and in the garden there was a new tomb ... [T]hey laid Jesus there (19:41-42). Consider also: 2:19,21.

Works cited

Brown, Raymond E., *The Gospel According to John*. Anchor Bible. 2 vols. Garden City, NY: Doubleday & Co., 1966 and 1970.

Brown, Raymond E., *A Crucified Christ in Holy Week*. Collegeville, Minnesota: The Liturgical Press, 1986.

Bultmann, Rudolf, *The Gospel of John: A Commentary*. English translation G.R. Beasley-Smith, et al. Oxford: Basil Blackwell, 1971.

Culpepper, R. Alan, *Anatomy of the Fourth Gospel: A Study in Literary Design*. Philadelphia: Fortress Press, 1983.

de la Potterie, Ignace, *The Hour of Jesus*. English translation Dom Gregory Murray. Slough: St Paul Publications, 1989.

Duke, Paul D., *Irony in the Fourth Gospel*. Atlanta: John Knox Press, 1985.

Ellis, Peter F., *The Genius of John*. Collegeville: Liturgical Press, 1984.

Flannery, Austin., ed., *Vatican Council II: The Conciliar and Post Conciliar Documents*. Northport, New York: Costello Publishing Company, 1975.

Forestell, J.T., *The Word of the Cross*. Anacleta Biblica #57. Rome: Biblical Institute Press, 1974.

Kaufman, Philip S., *The Beloved Disciple: witness against anti-Semitism*. Collegeville: Liturgical Press, 1991.

McHugh, J., 'The Glory of the Cross: The Passion According to St John.' *Clergy Review* 67 (1982), 117-27.

Meeks, Wayne A., *The Prophet-King: Moses Traditions and the Johannine Christology. Novum Testamentum* Supplement 14. Leiden: E.J. Brill, 1967.

Murphy-O'Connor, Jerome, *The Holy Land: An Archeological Guide from Earliest Times to 1700*. Second edition. Oxford and New York: Oxford University Press, 1986.

Navone, John, and Thomas Cooper, *The Story of the Passion*. Rome: Editrice Pontificia Universita Gregoriana, 1986.

Paul VI, Pope, *Marialis Cultus*. London: Catholic Truth Society, 1974.

Teilhard de Chardin, Pierre, *The Phenomenon of Man*. London: Collins Fount, 1977.